Too Scared of Tomorrow

A Clinical Approach to Understanding Fear

John Attram, PhD

authorHOUSE®

AuthorHouse™
1663 Liberty Drive
Bloomington, IN 47403
www.authorhouse.com
Phone: 1-800-839-8640

Published by AuthorHouse 1/16/2013

ISBN: 978-1-4817-0899-9 (sc)
ISBN: 978-1-4817-0898-2 (e)

TABLE OF CONTENTS

ACKNOWLEDGEMENTS

This project was made possible by the motivation from my children: Goddy, John, Martha, Michael, and Martin. The support I received from my dear friends Grace Muchiru, Hussein Ejiet, Supi Kobina Adams, David Kamutwe, and Julius Ndigwe reminded me that support comes in various forms, each of which is very necessary. Without the guidance of Drs. Auxier, Cabanilla, and O'Mara, members of the committee that supervised my dissertation, this book would not exist now. The greatest contributions in making this book possible are from the eleven men who trusted me and shared their experiences of abandonment with me. To all of these individuals and many others who want to remain anonymous, I say thank you.

INTRODUCTION

This book is intended to serve as a psychotherapy guide for clinicians working with individuals who hold back from trying to start new relationships because they harbor a worry that they will be rejected, be abandoned, fail, or even die. It is also meant to assist readers to get more in touch with their own feelings by reading about experiences and feelings of others who have faced loss and abandonment at important stages of their development. Using an interview approach, the author solicited stories of loss or abandonment from eleven men who grew up in fatherless families. Each chapter is a story of the experience of loss or abandonment which contributes to an understanding of innate fear as it emanates from such experience. This approach ties in with John W. Creswell's assertion that phenomenological inquiry probes human existence in detail because it gives access to subjective experiences that allow researchers to describe intimate aspects of people's lives (Creswell 2007). (All citations are to sources listed in the references section of this work.)

Fear of rejection holds people back from forming new friendships or relationships because it reduces the individual's self-esteem and confidence. Rejection, abandonment, and failure can cause so much difficulty in the mind because we often tie rejection to abstract ideas such as humiliation; inadequacy; uselessness; losing; not being good enough; being pathetic, all of which causes even more distress. When we dwell negatively upon an instance of rejection, it becomes harder for us to muster the courage to face another occasion in which we might get rejected again. Rejection is often much more troubling to those people who are very emotionally sensitive, who have low self-esteem, or who have had a very dysfunctional or abusive childhood. Initially, when individuals experience the emotional responses of injury, shame, and grief, which include denial, anxiety, fear, depression, anger, guilt or pride they hide their hurt inside. Often these self-protective hiding patterns are learned during childhood. The problem is that when people hide, they isolate themselves from the very things they need in order to heal and mature. What served as protection for a child becomes a prison for an adult.

This book highlights the experiences of eleven men who lived through abandonment and desertion from the very people who should have provided them with love, care, and protection. Understanding the lived experiences of eleven men who grew up without their fathers will thoroughly help in exploring the hiding patterns that people develop in such situations and provide guidance toward the healing grace and truth that God has built into safe, connected relationships with Him and others. These experiences and responses to them are journeys of discovery toward healing, connecting relationships, and new freedom and joy in living.

Studies on children's development and well-being have documented the impact of fatherlessness for their development. Unlike children who grow up with both biological parents, fatherless children are more likely to engage in health-compromising behaviors such as drug and alcohol use, unprotected sex, and cigarette smoking; are less likely to graduate from high school and college; are more likely to experience teenage or non-marital pregnancy; have lower levels of psychological well-being; have lower earnings, and are more likely to be out of school and out of work. The majority of prisoners, juvenile detention inmates, high school dropouts, pregnant teenagers, adolescent murderers, and rapists come from fatherless homes (National Fatherhood Initiative, 1996).

Whether caused by divorce and broken families, extramarital birth, cohabitation, or by deliberate single parenting, the incidence of fatherlessness is pervasive. According to Ventura and Barchrach (2000), one third of all births in the United States occur outside marriage. Recent statistics show that 85 per cent of single parent families in the United States are fatherless (Kreider & Fields, 2005). Most of these families are products of out-of-wedlock births and cohabitation. Additionally, studies show that 5.4 million children in 2001 lived with a biological mother who was not married to her partner (Bodenhorn, 2007).Rohner and Veneziano (2004) found that children from single parent homes had more physical and mental health problems than children who lived with two married parents. The increase of the phenomenon disconnects the structure of the modern family, making it a threat to modern human development. Some scholars do not believe that the negative social pathology associated with fatherless children is necessarily due to the absence of fathers in children's lives (Hubner & Ratzan, 2009), but believe that such effects are due to a host of secondary causes connected to the absence.

O'Neill and Hill (2003) pointed to socioeconomic variables, such as low income, parental education, and urban setting, in addition to single motherhood as major factors that caused fatherlessness in African American families. A combination of increased father involvement and closeness might be important in buffering adolescents from distress and from engaging in delinquent behaviors.

The connection between fatherlessness and crime is stronger than the relationships between race and crime and between low income and crime (Kamark and Gaston 1990). An examination of fatherlessness in contextual, qualitative research by this author defined themes associated with the experiences of fatherlessness and the meanings that fatherless children, particularly sons, attach to these experiences.

In this book, the stories of these eleven men will offer clinicians new insight into their own clients' reactions to abandonment and loss. This work will also guide clinicians and their clients to intervene in situations of fear of various things as a result of abandonment. Each chapter on a different fatherless man provides a personal narrative derived from in-depth interviews and shown in first-person language. Each chapter also has the author's explanation of the personal narratives, composite structural interpretations of the personal narratives, which are combined accounts of the personal narratives and the author's interpretation of the interview data that revealed the men experienced deeper emotions that they had not learned to own and express.

Due to their experiences of loss and abandonment, these men find it difficult to chart paths of growth which the author interprets as spiritual journeys. Spiritual journeys are inner journeys that each person must make on their own. Although many external resources, such as family, friends, religion, or spiritual practices, can provide support along the way, the journey itself is the sole work of the individual.

In chapter 12, a phenomenological interpretation of the eleven stories is provided along with a discussion of the constant themes that emerged from the eleven men's descriptions of their life experiences. In this book, the names of the men who were interviewed have been altered to preserve their anonymity.

CHAPTER 1
Garcon

I have been searching for my father from as early as when I was four years old. He was very close to me, so when he left without telling me anything, I was devastated. He did not tell my mother either. It seemed like he vanished into thin air. At the age of four years old, I came back from school and my father was not home. His clothes were there, but he was not home. My mother told me he might have gone to see his friends as usual, but, after several days when he did not return, I knew he was gone. At first, I felt something bad had happened to him, but when my aunt told us that he was living with another woman in another town, my mother asked me to forget about him. I tried, but I could not forget about my father.

The sense of loss that I experienced at that time led me to have faith in God. I came to accept my father's desertion because of my belief in God. I believed that God provided me with the assurance that I was not going to be abandoned again. Even though I was shocked, confused, powerless, and disconnected when my father left, I learned very early in life to be strong.

As a child, I hid the fact of my father's desertion; it seemed to me that I was the cause of that action. I kept looking for him in other father figures.

I succumbed to pressure from peers and used substances in my adolescence. I engaged in gang activities because I thought they gave me a sense of attachment. I used alcohol in college just to be counted among the "boys."

My mother sacrificed a lot for my upbringing. After my father left, she learned to become a receptionist at the bank. She did not have enough money, but she bought a house and tried to provide for my needs. She did not marry again, but she engaged in many abusive relationships that made her depressed and sad. Her choices of men made her unstable, but she told me that she also had been abandoned by her father, whose father also abandoned her grandmother when they came from Europe as immigrants. Those stories scared me, but I am committed to fathering my children. I hated those men who took advantage of my mother's vulnerability. I felt that all men, not just my father, were abusive to their spouses.

I did not know my father's brothers, but my mother had two brothers who were distant from us. I hardly saw them, and I did not know my cousins. The only male figures that were close to me impacted my life in negative ways: Mom's boyfriends, who were alcohol users and acted in very mean ways; the leaders of the gang that I joined as an adolescent; and my close friends with whom I hung out for a long time but who taught me how to use drugs and alcohol. My pastor and the members of the men's fellowship have provided me with positive insights into life and have turned my life around.

My father's sister used to visit us when I was a child, but when my father left, she hardly visited us. She knew where my father was but she could not take me to him. I did not know any of my grandparents. They were gone before I was born.

Having been raised by my mother, I view women as the custodians of children. However, it all depends on their financial situation.

Women need partners that are trustworthy and caring to sustain their relationships. Without a father, it becomes very difficult for a woman to go it alone. Women are committed to their children no matter what, so they would do anything for them, but they really need a helping hand from the father. I am committed to my wife and my children. I respect my colleagues at work, women in the church, and all women, because fathers may go away, but mothers are devoted and committed to their children.

Fathers are important for the well-being of their children. It is not a matter of money, but their involvement in the child's life ensures that the child does well in school and develops in positive ways without behavioral or emotional problems. Fathers need to be active in the lives of their children. They should serve as role models for their sons, so they have to exhibit good character and responsible behavior for their children to follow.

I missed these and many other opportunities in life. My addiction with drugs and alcohol abated as a result of God's grace. Otherwise, without the guidance of a father, I would have been a useless man by now. I am thankful to my church elders for providing me with the safety and protection from drug dependence and addiction.

I wish my father would return to me. I miss him. I miss his voice. I would have gone in search of him, but I am afraid of another rejection from him. For example, when his sister refused to send me to my father, I felt a sense of rejection. Also, the alienation my mother and I faced from my father's family was very deep. My mother acknowledged the other day that she did nothing wrong to warrant my father's desertion, so it seemed to me the fault was mine. If he feels guilty for abandoning us, he should know that I have forgiven him. I want him back in my life.

Generally, I have a positive way of thinking about myself. I feel good both at work and in the community. I take a positive view of the world, hoping that if I try hard, I will succeed in all that I do.

My mother was able to provide me with my needs, but I consider the positive male interactions and the financial contributions from my church as beneficial to my adult development and the future life chances that I have. As a mentor in the church, I am hopeful that my involvement with the youth will foster positive developmental outcomes for these kids as they grow up. My work has also been associated with positive aspects of adult children's educational attainment, relationship quality, and career success.

I don't see myself different from other kids. I am capable of doing what every man can do. I have already learned my life lessons. I have made my mistakes and with the help of other role models, I have corrected them. I only need to get rid of my fears and move on in confidence.

My wife understands where I am coming from. She supports me in everything I do. She believes that I am always going to be a good father to my children.

My mother visits me regularly. We have the best bond. I love my mom and she trusts and respects me. She encourages me to take good care of my family and be present for them, support them, and be a responsible man.

I have few friends because of my past experiences. Friends come in many shapes and sizes and I am careful in whatever I say to my peers. My focus is on my job and my mentoring work in the church. I command respect from both my colleagues and supervisors.

Structural Interpretation of Garcon's Lived Experience

For many years, Garcon lived with anxious feelings due to the painful memory of his father's sudden desertion in his childhood. He coped with this pain by constantly hoping that one day his father would show up again in his life. He also depended on his mother's support to survive those difficult times, because she was the only person who understood and shared his pain. Furthermore, he looked for his father in surrogates that led him to an association with gangs and other people who used drugs. These connections did not provide him comfort but instead increased his pain. Finally, his search led him to turn to other sources of support and authority to replace the loss of his father, and this shift allowed him to cope with his hurt. With a pervasive belief in God, Garcon received solace and safety from his church elders and members who assured him that he was not going to be abandoned again.

Depending on his mother's strength and willpower, Garcon learned to be strong and resilient in the face of adversity. He was committed to fathering his children and maintaining a successful marriage. He ascribed his peaceful nature to his mother, who had gone through hardships because of the wrong choices she made in her own life but who also sacrificed greatly for his growth. Garcon's mother herself was abandoned by her father, and her grandfather had also walked out on her grandmother. This trend served as a source of anxiety for Garcon. He was anxious about the burden that was on him to break this intergenerational cycle and to gain an understanding of why fathers desert their children. His mother's parental abandonment served as an additional sense of loss for him.

The lack of positive role models in his life served as a source of mistrust for Garcon. He did not trust the men who took advantage of his mother, and this was manifested in his empathetic feelings toward women and scorn for men. Though he knew that he needed a male father figure in his life to protect him and guide him, he did not look to the males in his family or his mother's acquaintances to fill that role.

From his experience, he believed that these men served as negative role models on whom he could not depend. Additionally, from his interactions with gangs, Garcon had confirmed the destructive and doubtful nature of such surrogate figures. With his newfound belief in God, he depended on the support from members of his church to fill that vacuum in his life.

Garcon felt that there was something wrong with his personality that made his father leave and never come back; therefore he continued to search for his father to gain an insight into why he abandoned him. He also thought that like the other men his mother brought home, his father was not competent enough to maintain a lasting relationship with him. Furthermore, he felt that his mother might have done something wrong to warrant his father's deserting her. These unanswered questions pestered his mind, and he sought answers for them. His anxiety feelings were the result of not knowing what was on his father's mind.

These early life experiences led to continuing irrational fears in the present. He knew it was important to gain an insight into why his father left. He had verbalized it many times, but he feared that if he found his father, the man might reject him. This fear made him anxious in continuing with his search, because succeeding in it might give him additional pain.

Composite Interpretation of Garcon's Lived Experience

Garcon's emotional response to his experience of can be interpreted by the following themes:

Confusion. For many years, Garcon lived with anxious feelings due to the painful memory of his father's sudden desertion in his childhood. ("The alienation my mother and I faced from my father's family was very deep.") His anxiety feelings were driven by a profound emotion of confusion from not knowing why his father left and from the memories of the relationship he shared with his father in his early childhood. ("It seemed like he vanished into thin air.") His father's sudden disappearance was a source of great concern to Garcon because there was no quarrel between his parents and he did not believe his father just went away. Thus, he supposed that it might be his fault. ("My mother acknowledged the other day that she did nothing wrong to warrant my father's desertion, so it seemed to me the fault was mine.") He wondered how his father could have left without giving him a hint of what was going on, since he was close to his father in many respects. This made him confused because his father used to take him to school and he believed his father loved him. ("He was very close to me, so when he left without telling me anything, I was devastated.")

He felt unwanted and alienated and wanted to get an understanding of what might have triggered his father's desertion. Depending on his mother's support, he was able to cope with this pain, hoping that one day his father would show up again in his life. ("I tried, but how could I forget about my father?") He was anxious to know what had happened to his father, yet there was no one to help him find his father.

Loneliness. Garcon searched for his father in surrogates that led him to an association with gangs and other people who used drugs. ("I have been searching for my father from as early as when I was four years old. ... I kept looking for him in other father figures.") These connections did not provide him comfort, but rather increased his pain. ("I engaged in gang activities because I thought they gave me a sense of attachment.") But the connections also served as avenues for him to replace his thoughts of the loss of his father. ("I succumbed to pressure from peers to use substances in my adolescence.") He engaged in all these activities so that he could gain an insight into why his father left and whether he would ever come back. Garcon believed that getting an understanding of why his father left would ease his anxiety and doubt of not knowing.

With his pervasive religious belief, Garcon sought solace in his church as a way of searching for what he had lost. ("The sense of loss that I experienced led me to have faith in God.") Searching for his father led him to turn to other sources of support and authority to replace his loss, a shift that helped him to cope with his hurt. Due to an imbued faith in God, Garcon received solace and safety from his church's elders and members who assured him that he was not going to be abandoned again. ("My pastor and the members of the men's fellowship have provided me with positive insights into life.") He wondered if having a better understanding of his father will allow him to better understand himself. ("Fathers need to be active in the lives of their children. They should serve as role models for their sons, so they have to exhibit good character and responsible behavior for their children to follow.")

Shame. As a child and an adolescent, Garcon tried to hide the fact that his father deserted him, as though it was his fault. ("As a child, I hid the fact of my father's desertion; it seemed to me that I was the cause of that action.") His search for his father in different alliances was a result of the shame he harbored within him. He grieved that his peers with whom he was close had their fathers in their lives, but the real cause of his grief was the shame that he felt when he was among his peers. ("I don't see myself different from other kids. ... I have already learned my life lessons.")

Garcon's alliance with his church members offered him some self-confidence. ("I am thankful to my church elders for providing me with the safety and protection from drug dependence and addiction.") It also impacted his life in positive ways. ("My pastor and the members of the men's fellowship have provided me with positive insights into life.") And these insights built within him strength to move on in life.

Hurt. Garcon demonstrated anger at the individuals who influenced him in negative ways. ("The only male figures that were close to me impacted my life in negative ways.") He was especially angry with his father for deserting him and his mother because he believed that his life would have been positively different if his biological father had played a part in it. ("He was very close to me, so when he left without telling me anything, I was devastated.") ("He did not tell my mother either.") Garcon believed that his father could have developed a better place for him in life where he could have chosen a better career path and led a better life. ("Fathers are important for the well-being of their children.")

Whenever he saw his friends with their fathers, he was hurt. ("I missed these and many other opportunities in life.")

He was angry with his boyfriends of his mom because they reminded him of his association with the gang leaders and his peers who taught him drug use. ("Mom's boyfriends were alcohol users and acted in very mean ways, just like the leaders of the gang that I joined as an adolescent.")

By and large, his anger was born out of the hurt of not knowing where his father was and why there was no positive alternative in his place.

Vulnerability. Garcon blamed his abandonment experiences on the intergenerational transmission of the phenomenon in his mother's family. His mother's wrong choices of male partners were the result of being abandoned by her father. She had been searching for a father figure all her life too. As he was reminded of his mother's experiences, Garcon feared that he would continue with the intergenerational cycle

9

himself. ("Her choices of men made her unstable, but she told me that she also had been abandoned by her father, whose father also abandoned her grandmother.") He felt vulnerable in the face of his mother's traumatic family problem, and his sense of vulnerability increased with the thought that there was a likelihood the pattern would continue. ("Those stories scared me, but I am committed to fathering my children; I hated those men.")

Seeking to break that cycle, Garcon was always there for his children and other children in his community. But he was also afraid for his children and the children of others in his church and his community. ("I am committed to my wife and children. … As a mentor in the church, I am hopeful that my involvement with the youth will foster positive developmental outcomes for these kids as they grow up.")

He described his feelings of vulnerability that were born out of the fear that he might be rejected again if he found his father. ("I would have gone in search of him, but I am afraid of another rejection from him.")

CHAPTER 2
Leon

I had traumatic childhood experiences. My mother and I lived in a one-bedroom apartment in the big city. My uncle, my mother's older brother, used to visit us at the end of every other week and bring us food. Mother did not bring food home, but most nights she left me alone in our room, returning the next morning. I asked my mother why she always left me alone, but she told me that she had to work to get us food to eat.

She told me how she came into that job. Mom talked at length about how her stepfather sexually abused her when she was a teenager. She said she had to work in a liquor house and got pregnant with me at the age of 16. She told me that she had to sit on the laps of men who were old enough to be her father, but she was forced to do it in order to get paid. Mom told me that when she got pregnant, she informed her boyfriend who was her regular sex partner, but he beat her up and told her that he was not responsible for the pregnancy. She said her mother had then thrown her out of the house after her mother found her having sex with her stepfather. Mother ran away to the city, gave birth, and rented our apartment.

After I was born, Mother entered into full time prostitution. My mother's friends were prostitutes too. They came to our room, smoked marijuana, and formulated their solicitation plans for the next night.

When I was twelve years old, my mother's brother came to take me to his house because my mother had been arrested and sent to jail for engaging in prostitution and drugs. This uncle was a drug peddler. He had been to jail several times for drug problems. Each week, the police came to our neighborhood in search of drug dealers and users. My uncle had guns and pistols in his room, but he told me not to touch them.

When I was fourteen years old, my uncle was jailed for six years for armed robbery. He left behind a bag of marijuana in his bedroom. As my uncle was serving his jail term, I sold the drugs that he left behind to make a living. I got a lot of money to buy fancy clothes. I went to the liquor house at night and took home prostitutes to sleep with. It was a good life then. I dropped out of school at the eighth grade and got myself more marijuana from the dealers to sell. I used one of my uncle's pistols to protect myself. I also gave one of his guns to an older man who served as my bodyguard.

When my uncle was discharged from prison, I thought he was going to be mad at me for selling his drugs, but he was happy that I had grown to be a big boy with a lot of money. I gave him some money to restart his life, and we moved to a bigger house where we sold drugs and acted as pimps for prostitutes.

My family was stigmatized by the many incarcerations of my cousins and uncles. As long as I could remember, the males from my family were all in prison. My mother's stepfather was jailed for life after he was charged with murdering my grandmother. Two of my mother's brothers were in jail for criminal charges, and all my cousins had been in jail several times in their lives for various drug offenses. Until I grew up, it seemed to me that jail was a good place to be. I can remember telling my friend in grade school that I had a lot of relatives in jail, but she explained to me that prison was for bad people.

One day, I was arrested for possessing a dangerous weapon. My uncle got me a good lawyer; therefore I was jailed for only one year. As I was entering prison, my mother was getting out of jail, but she was able to visit me a couple of times. She had changed, and she told me she would pray to God to protect me.

In prison, I found a mentor who told me that the only way to stay out of trouble was to learn a trade. He was a corrections officer who took me to church and encouraged me to learn how to cut hair. Barbering was interesting, so I underwent an apprenticeship with a master barber who taught me the trade with which I now earn my living.

I don't think I had a family. I knew two of my mother's sisters, but they were different from my mother. One of them was a teacher, and the other was married and lived with her husband back in our hometown. But they hardly spoke to us.

There have not been female family members in my life. My aunts did not play any role in my childhood development. The other females I knew were my mother's prostitute friends and my uncle's many girlfriends. We had a casual relationship. Females have not had any influence on my life, but I respect them. I will respect my girlfriend when I get one. My grandmother was murdered when I was a kid. I did not know her a lot. My uncle told me that my grandma was a strong woman, but unfortunately they all disobeyed her. She married the wrong man who abused her and her children and killed her when she wanted out of the marriage.

Apart from the time she was in jail, my mother has always shown me love. She visited me in prison and encouraged me to be a better person.

My mother was put in her situation by her stepfather who abused her and killed her mother. That man was evil, and the consequences of his actions have been transmitted to most of my family members. I know that if it were not for his actions, I would have known my father. My mother could have had a home and gone to school. She would not have gone to the liquor houses. She would have been married before getting pregnant. I would have known my father. I would have known my grandmother. My aunts would have stayed with us and there would have been peace in our family. That was the devil that destroyed all our lives.

If fathers would be allowed to marry their children's mothers, many of us would not be fatherless. I don't blame black fathers who run away from their families. They are poor, uneducated, and discriminated against. In most cases, the effects of poverty, illiteracy, and discrimination send most black men to jail when they try to do things that will give them money to turn their lives around and become responsible for their families. Coming out of jail, the black man becomes hopeless and bitter. Their children bear the brunt of these unfair social arrangements.

Having known this, I will take my time to find a good woman to marry, so that I would love her and live together with my children as a family. I suffered a lot to get here, but it was not my fault. It was not my mother's fault, neither was it my father's fault. They were all running away from a situation that they could do nothing about. But no matter how poor, uneducated, or lowly placed a father is, he should take care of his children.

As a child, I missed everything, but I did not care. After all, most of my friends did not have fathers. I had fun on my own, so I find it difficult to get along well with my peers who had fathers in their lives.

Next week I am going for my GED. I want to be a better person. I still have time.

When I was in prison, I learned one thing, that is, those men were reduced to low-class human beings. Most of them were very smart guys, but their independence had been seized. They were not respected by the officers, and I know when they come out they will have a hard time to gain their confidence back. I believed in what one corrections officer told me: "The only way to stay out of trouble is to learn a trade." A positive self-image means gaining a high self-esteem. Men should stay out of drugs and alcohol and be educated. The girls will love you and your kids will have confidence in you.

If my father had accepted me, I believe that I would not have gone to jail. My uncle did his best, but in the wrong way. My father would not have allowed me to do drugs. Anyway, I think I should learn to forget about my traumatic childhood experiences as much as I can, so that I can move on with my life.

I have forgiven my father. Maybe he is somewhere in jail, or he may be dead. I don't know. But I have forgiven him. He was a coward for not owning up to his responsibilities. As for me, I would "man up" when the time comes and be there for my wife and kids. I envy those kids who have fathers, but there are not many of them in my circles. Most of my friends have no fathers. With all that I went through, with no one to positively guide and mentor me, I think it is a privilege to have a father.

Now I liken my childhood experiences to a child crawling toward a fireplace. He needs a mother or a father to stop him from getting hurt, but I had no one like that, so I got hurt.

I know myself. I don't care what others think about me, but I see myself as a good guy. It's simply that I did not have a good chance in life. It is only by God's grace that I have come this far. I still smoke marijuana because it makes me spiritual. It is the only thing that connects me to others in my circles; it's the father of the fatherless—ha ha ha. People respect me because I have great respect for my clients. Above all, I love my mother, who still cooks for me. I have no girlfriend, and as I told you, I will wait until I meet a good girl who I can marry.

Structural Interpretation of Leon's Lived Experience

Leon experienced trauma in his childhood as a result of being abandoned by his father even before he was born. Additionally, he suffered increased pain from his mother's irresponsible parenting behavior. Without her having a steady sexual partner, it was easy for the man whom she thought was responsible for her pregnancy to deny and abandon her. While Leon's narrative does not mention it, Leon informed me that he became extremely angry when he learned from his mother that she had to solicit for men, after her stepfather raped her, in order to feed herself. This knowledge was an additional source of confusion for him, because he believed that he would never know who his father was since his mother had multiple sexual partners at the time he was conceived.

He also believed that his mother's childhood experiences influenced his own, because his mother was rejected by her own mother when it was found that she was sexually molested by her stepfather. Leon, however, did not blame his mother, because it was not her fault. Rather, he blamed his step-grandfather who sexually abused her when she just sixteen years old.

Leon's childhood experiences included the pain of going through hunger and loneliness most of the time. Most nights his mother left him alone, without food or a caregiver, and she went out to engage in drinking and prostituting. He had known earlier that his mother worked at liquor houses as a lap dancer and a prostitute, as a result of which she got pregnant without a steady partner. The shame of this knowledge, coupled with his mother's inability to care for him properly, caused Leon a lot of grief. Without any peers in his life, he felt rejected because there was no one to whom he could look for support. When his mother left for the city to find work, Leon thought things were going to change for the better. Life in the city became stressful, however, because his mother hardly ever came back home to him.

He spent many nights alone in their room. He was also exposed to drug use by his mother and her friends. These experiences resulted in an intense emotional response of fear, helplessness, and discomfort. Eventually, Leon's mother was arrested for substance use and prostitution. As she was going to jail, she asked her brother, who was also a drug peddler, to take good care of her twelve-year-old son. Her decision was destructive for Leon's future. In his uncle's house, Leon learned to use drugs and weapons.

At first he enjoyed the reckless, adventure-seeking life of drug use and peddling since it gave him excitement, fun, and a sense of living on the edge. But when he was arrested for possessing drugs and dangerous weapons and was jailed for a year, Leon came to terms with reality-based thought processes. His life of impulsive reactivity was a source of pain that defined his present life. Leon had known about imprisonment when he was a little boy because his cousins and uncles had been imprisoned at one time or another for drug and other offenses. He conceived of it as a standard stage in life. But he later realized that this stage was highly disruptive, one that constrained the possibility of attaining other standard stages of his life such as completing his education and obtaining a stable employment.

In prison, Leon learned a trade. He found a role model in a corrections officer who advised him to stay out of trouble by learning a trade. He took his apprenticeship seriously and got certified as a professional barber.

Leon was angry with everybody around him. He acknowledged that he was angry with his father, whom he had forgiven. He blamed his lack of education and lack of family ties on the social system. He believed that African Americans were discriminated against and that this influenced their way of life. Leon was angry with his present social status, which he described as the consequence of the incarceration of his family members.

Though he blamed his step-grandfather for raping his mother and murdering his grandmother, Leon believed that his step-grandfather was a victim of a system that frustrated African American men to the point that they engaged in criminal activities. He was angry because he believed that the effects of poverty, illiteracy, and discrimination caused his mother to engage in illicit activities just like he believed any black woman would do in those conditions.

Leon believed that he and his mother were alienated by their family. The resulting sense of loss from this served as a source of anger toward his mother's sisters. He was not in touch with his aunts and he hardly knew anything about his dead grandmother, who had disclaimed his mother and sent her away. His uncle, who was the closest relative he knew, did not provide him with the positive example he needed. He felt very lonely when he thought about the lack of important attachment figures in his life. The abandonment wound inflicted on him was a source of insecurity that led to toxic feelings that made him apprehensive to marry or engage in intimate relationships. The center of this wound was an insatiable need for love that he continued to look for.

He acknowledged that at age 25, he had no girlfriend, because of what he learned in his childhood.

He understood the negative effects of the use of drugs, yet he believed that drug use was the only way he could connect to his peers. Leon believed that individuals who use drugs end up with stigma, shame, and hardship. He also believed that drug use reduced his mother to being a prostitute, reduced his uncle to an ex-convict with no hope for his life, and was responsible for Leon's own social discomfort and lack of self-esteem, yet he continued to use marijuana as his way of connecting with others.

Since he lacked the ability to understand the viewpoints of others, he felt he was misunderstood by others. He was hopeful that he would find someone who would understand him and marry him.

He was also hopeful that he would get his GED credential in order to improve his social status.

His denial and projection of blame for his responsibilities prevented him from coming to terms with the realities of his life.

Composite Interpretation of Leon's Lived Experience

Hurt. Leon's childhood experiences were filled with hurt because his father denied him even before he was born. ("Now I liken my childhood experiences to a child crawling toward a fireplace. He needs a mother or a father to stop him from getting hurt, but I had no one like that, so I got hurt." "I had traumatic childhood experiences.")

He was angry when he learned from his mother that she had to solicit for men in order to feed herself. He was also angry because during his childhood he hardly saw his mother. ("I asked my mother why she always left me alone. But she told me that she had to work to get us food to eat.") Yet she hardly ever came home and did not bring food home. ("Mother did not bring food home, but most nights she left me alone in our room, returning the next morning.") Furthermore, in addition to being hurt by his father's rejection, he did not understand why his mother was not in his life. The memory of his mother's behavior was a source of anger for him, but deep inside, he was hurt. ("My mother's friends were prostitutes too. They came to our room, smoked marijuana, and formulated their solicitation plans for the next night.") The memory of all these activities increased Leon's hurt, which he masked with anger.

Shame. Another source of pain for Leon was that his mother was raped by her stepfather. ("Mom talked at length about how her stepfather sexually abused her when she was a teenager.") The shame of this unholy act made him confused and angry, because he could not understand the rationale behind his step-grandfather's behavior. ("That man was evil, and the consequences of his actions have been transmitted to most of my family members.")

Leon was also ashamed at his mother's work in the liquor house, sitting on the laps of men to earn a living. ("She had to work in a liquor house after she got pregnant with me at the age of sixteen years old.")

Because of his mother's activities with men, he believed that he would never know who his father was, as his mother had multiple sexual partners at the time he was conceived. ("Mom told me that when she got pregnant, she informed her boyfriend who was her regular sex partner, but he beat her up and told her that he was not responsible for the pregnancy.") It became all too clear to Leon that his mother's behavior could not engender any meaningful relationship that would make any man own up for her pregnancy.

Another source of shame for Leon was that most of his family members had been to jail at one time or the other. ("My family was stigmatized by the many incarcerations of my cousins and uncles.") He felt guilty when he later understood that he helped to perpetuate the family stigma of multiple incarcerations.

Confusion. Leon's childhood experience of being among prostitutes and drug peddlers served as a source of confusion for him. ("My mother's friends were prostitutes; they came to our room, smoked marijuana, and formulated their solicitation plans for the next night.") He could not understand why his mother could not lead a good life. ("After I was born, Mother entered into full time prostitution.")

He also struggled with the knowledge that his grandmother deserted his mother very early in her life. ("She said her mother had then thrown her out of the house after she found her having sex with her stepfather.") He wondered if that caused her mother to live the way she did.

He was equally confused when his mother was arrested. He did not know what to do with his life first without a father and then without a mother. ("When I was twelve years old, my mother's brother came to take me to his house because my mother had been arrested and sent to jail.") Her decision was destructive for Leon's future. ("My uncle who came for me after my mother's incarceration was a drug peddler.") In his confused mind, Leon had no choice other than to enjoy the reckless, adventure-seeking life of drug use and peddling since it gave him excitement, fun, and a sense of living on the edge. ("As my uncle was serving his jail term, I sold the drugs that he left behind. It was a good life then.") Reality set in, however, when he was arrested for possessing drugs and dangerous weapons and was jailed for a year. His life of impulsive reactivity was a source of pain that defined his present life. ("As I was entering prison, my mother was getting out of jail.")

Having known about prison life through the experiences of his uncles and cousins at an early age, Leon thought prison was the only alternative place to live apart from the life of poverty and shame in the neighborhood. ("Until I grew up, it seemed to me that jail was a good place to be.") Since incarceration was commonplace in his neighborhood, Leon thought that life in prison was better than life in the neighborhood. ("I can remember telling my friend in grade school that I had a lot of relatives in jail.") He did not understand the outcome of being sent to jail for a young person like himself. He was confused with the real impact of prison and his perception of it. ("But she explained to me that prison was for bad people.")

Loneliness. In addition to losing his father even before he was born, Leon experienced multiple losses of significant people to incarceration in his childhood. His uncle, with whom he was very close, had been in and out of jail several times, but the incarceration that impacted his life was when he was fourteen years old. ("When I was fourteen years old, my uncle was jailed for six years for armed robbery.") His uncle's incarceration brought a lot of hardship on Leon because even though his uncle's life negatively impacted his own, his uncle was the only role model he knew. ("I don't think I had a family. I knew two of my mother's sisters, but they were different from my mother. One of them was a teacher, and the other was married and lived with her husband back in our hometown. But they hardly spoke to us.") The loneliness Leon felt was the result of the lack of connection with his close relatives. ("There have not been female family members in my life.")

Vulnerability. The deeper meaning of Leon's angry feelings was centered in the fear of continuing the dysfunctional dynamics in his family. ("That man was evil, and the consequences of his actions have been transmitted to most of my family members. I know that if it were not for his actions, I would have known my father. My mother could have had a home and gone to school. She would not have gone to the liquor houses. She would have been married before getting pregnant. I would have known my father. I would have known my grandmother. My aunts would have stayed with us and there would have been peace in our family. That was the devil that destroyed all our lives.")

His feelings of vulnerability increased with a fear that getting into any meaningful relationship was bound to fail. ("Having known this, I will take my time to find a good woman to marry, so that I would love her and live together with my children as a family.")

He was afraid of the situation his parents found themselves in. ("I suffered a lot to get here, but it was not my fault. It was not my mother's fault, neither was it my father's fault.") He felt that they were in places they could not help themselves out of. "They were all running away from a situation that they could do nothing about.")

As a result of the treatment he received at the hands of males—his father, his step-grandfather, his mother's boyfriends, and his uncle—Leon struggled to move into unfamiliar situations for fear of being taken advantage of. ("With all that I went through, with no one to positively guide and mentor me, I think it is a privilege to have a father.") His step grandfather sexually abused his mother; his mother's boyfriend beat her up when she confronted him with their pregnancy and rejected her at that critical time of her life and that of her unborn child. Leon was afraid to interact with his peers because he had been exposed to the adult life very early in life. He had to fend for himself when his mother was locked up and also when his uncle went to prison. ("I had fun on my own, and so I find it difficult to get along with my peers who had fathers in their lives.")

Though he respected females, he also had a fear of marrying any time soon, which stemmed from his mother's relationship difficulties and the abuse and rejection that the women in his childhood faced. ("I love my mother, who still cooks for me." "I will respect my girlfriend when I get one.") But Leon is cautious about marrying. ("I will wait until I meet a good girl who I can marry.")

Worthlessness: Leon felt humiliated by significant others in his developmental years, so he carried significant doubts about his traits and abilities to perform tasks and take on new responsibilities. ("Now I liken my childhood experiences to a child crawling toward a fireplace. He needs a mother or a father to stop him from getting hurt, but I had no one like that, so I got hurt.")

Leon thought that he was shameful, that he was defective, unworthy, and unlovable, so his use of marijuana served as a defense that his ego utilized to help him survive his childhood pain.

He hoped, however, to redeem himself, because he felt worthless in the face of the difficulties he faced after his incarceration. ("Next week I am going for my GED. I want to be a better person. I still have time.")

He believed that he could change his self-worth as a human being but wondered how best he could do that. ("I know myself. I don't care what others think about me but I see myself as a good guy.") He believed that he was a smart person with a lot of potential but that his ability to make use of his innate skills had been taken away by his record of incarceration. ("When I was in prison, I learned one thing, that is, those men were reduced to low-class human beings. Most of them were very smart guys, but their independence had been seized.") Leon acknowledged that he was going to find it difficult to gain his self-worth, but he was ready to do his best to become a better person. ("They were not respected by the officers and I know when they come out they will have a hard time to gain their confidence back.") He believed that young people should be hopeful and stay out of crime and drugs, because to him that is the only way to stay out of trouble and gain self-confidence. ("A positive self-image means gaining a high self-esteem. Men should stay out of drugs and alcohol and be educated. The girls will love you and your kids will have confidence in you.")

From his narrative, I concluded that Leon kept looking for father figures but could not find one among his immediate family members. ("My uncle who came for me after my mother's incarceration was a drug peddler. He had been in jail many times for drug problems.") Leon finally found a positive male role model when he was in jail, but the harm had already been done to his life. ("I believed in what one corrections officer told me: 'The only way to stay out of trouble is to learn a trade.'")

CHAPTER 3
Lawrence

Hmm ... where do I begin? I have known about my father all my life, but I met him for the first time when I was twenty-eight years old. I am not sure why and when he decided that he would not be part of my life, but my mother single-handedly raised me. When it became apparent to me that my mother did not want me to contact my father, I was wounded and felt unsafe. Even though I always had a sincere interest in contacting my biological father someday, I was honestly afraid of hurting my mother's feelings and I was afraid my father might reject me if I did. I simply did not know how I would deal with the rejection.

What I know about my early childhood is that my parents were married before I was born. I remember my father driving me to school on my first day and then every day. When Mama began to take me, I asked her why, and she said my dad had left. I asked her so many questions that she got angry and told me not to talk about my father again.

When I was about eight years old, Mama told me she had divorced my father because they did not get along well. She promised that she was going to take good care of me.

I kept a lot of pictures of my father in my room. I looked at them each day, but I also longed to see him, talk to him, and ask him questions.

When I was in high school, I played basketball and football. It was only my mother who attended my games and encouraged me. I wanted to meet my father to get answers to the questions that plagued my mind. I wanted to know why he never visited me or attended my basketball games. I wanted to know if he loved me and if he was willing to be in my life. I felt I was doing this for myself, and this time, if he rejected me, I would deal with it.

I think something happened to me in school that brought me to the guidance and counseling office. It became clear to me at that time that I was angry for no apparent reason; my grades had taken a dip, and I thought of dropping out of school. I felt I missed my father. My mother was informed, but she did not take me to my dad.

When I went to college, I was so busy with my studies and other extracurricular activities that I forgot about my father. I did well in college and got a good job after that. On my twenty-eighth birthday, my girlfriend threw a party for me and we decided to invite my father. I did not tell my mother about the invitation because I felt it was time for me to make my own decisions. You can imagine the excitement of meeting my father for the first time after twenty-three years. This started the beginning of our new relationship.

There were so many intriguing things about my father. He was so kind and wonderful. There was an instant connection. We looked alike, and after a long conversation, I realized that we had similar personality traits. My mother was surprised to see how excited I was with my father. I never realized how much I cared about a man I hardly knew. He had driven me to school when I was a child. That was the only contact we had—but here I am being closely drawn to him. How could this be? I questioned myself about how I was feeling. I wondered if I could have a bond with a man that did not play a part in my upbringing. Our relationship has continued to develop slowly through emails and more visits. We have bonded nicely. I have even forgotten he was not there most of my life.

When I was growing up, my mother's brother, who was a pastor, visited us on important occasions, but he hardly stayed. He was a busy man. My uncle always asked my mother to let me visit him when school was on break, but Mother would not let me go. I looked up to my uncle as a positive role model. He advised me to take my studies seriously and always asked me what I wanted to be in the future.

My mother's boyfriend who lived in our house for a while was not the type I wanted as a role model. He was a good man, but I felt he was using my mother, because my mother did only what this man wanted. She hardly paid attention to me when he was present, so I did not like him. In a way, he was responsible for my mother's hatred for my father. Because her boyfriend was always there, my mother did not want me to talk about my father. My mother never got to do what she wanted to do. For example, once she wanted to buy a particular car, but her boyfriend dissuaded her into buying something else. He was controlling and short-tempered. I was scared that these traits could turn into mental abuse for my mother, who gave a lot to please him, while he seemed to give very little back.

My mother's sisters were wonderful people. They took me to their houses whenever I came back from school. I bonded very well with my cousins. One of my aunts, who was a teacher, ensured that we all understood the need to be strong and not to fall for peer pressure. She taught us about how to solve our problems and be respectful of other people's opinions. At first, I thought my aunties were controlling, but as I was growing up I found their advice useful.

The most important female family member in my life was my late grandmother. Grandma was the pillar of our family. She attended every baptism, confirmation, and graduation ceremony of her grandchildren.

She gave us gifts, especially at Christmas. She was very caring, but I did not understand why my mother did not allow me to stay with Grandma for a while when she asked her. Grandma loved me. She visited me when I was in college and gave me money. She even gave some money to my roommate. Grandma was good.

Having been raised by my mother, I feel I owe females due respect and affection. Females are very loving and caring, especially when one reciprocates their love. I love my wife and my female colleagues. In this way, they also respect me and value my worth. Women should be treated with respect. When I hear stories about men abusing women, I conclude that those men were mentally disturbed. I would never raise a finger on a woman, no matter what.

Fathers are the custodians of the family. My father left when I was a child, so I did not experience his protection and care. Fathers need to be patient with mothers and try to solve problems between them so that the kids are not affected. I still don't know why my parents divorced, because neither of them wanted to talk about it. It's a problem that they decided to keep secret, and I respect that. However, as the Bible admonished fathers to be heads of their families, they should exercise restraint when they are breaking away—especially when there are kids involved. I don't blame my mother or my father for my growing up fatherless, but I would not want my children to grow up without me. Fathers should put in place the necessary insurance protections so that in their absence their children will not suffer. But they should endeavor to be physically present for them, play with them, discipline them when they go wrong, and take them to church. Oh yes.

I missed my father when it came to going to school with my mother. I missed him when my mother's boyfriend refused to answer some of my questions. My mother's boyfriend was not ready to commit to their relationship because he was not willing to take up the fathering role.

He was only there for my mother and not for me. My father's presence in my life would have made a huge difference.

We now have a wonderful relationship. My father was afraid of my mother; that was why he hardly visited me. I love my father. Whatever happened between him and my mother caused him to stay away. He is a wonderful man. Even though he has not explained why he went away, I forgive him. He was at my college graduation and my wedding. When I was thirty years old, he threw a big party at his house for me. There, I met my two sisters and my youngest brother, who looked just like me.

I believe that a positive self-image is having a strong character, not succumbing to pressures from your peers, and resolving conflicts as they come. To me, a positive self-image means giving out to others what you have and what you know. I preach at a local Sunday school and I derive great joy from it.

I thank God for getting me through my teenage and adolescent years without many problems. It might have been through the guidance of my mother, aunts, and my grandmother. They were always there to offer advice and counseling. My father seemed to me a wonderful person who would have played his fatherly role in a positive way, but he was not there. It was not his fault. My mother kept him away, but now that we are together, we are both making the best out of our time.

My mother gave me everything that I needed. As a child, I definitely missed those times that other kids had their fathers at their games, but Mom was there too. I was not different from those kids. I was friends with most of them and none asked me about my dad.

I try my best to be a good example to others. I support my wife and son in every way. My mother is proud of my traits and accomplishments. I wish my grandma was alive to see how well I have grown into a man. She would have been proud too. I serve as a positive role model to my cousins and nephews. I think others will describe me in positive terms.

Structural Interpretation of Lawrence's Lived Experience

Lawrence knew about his father all his life, so he struggled with the pain of verbalizing how his father suddenly left him and his mother. His earlier happiness of being driven to school each morning by his father turned to grief after his father left. He did not understand the reason behind his father leaving, and his mother hardly talked about it. Lawrence could not express his feelings to others because he was hurt. He kept searching for his father in his mind for a long time. In addition to his pain of being abandoned by his father, he did not know how to go about seeking contact with his father, because he did not know how his mother would react to it if she knew or how his father would respond if Lawrence found him. His fear of being rejected made Lawrence keep his search for his father a secret.

He lived with his pain until four years later when his mother revealed to him the cause of their divorce, even though she did not give him the details. She only indicated that they did not get on well, and she promised to take good care of Lawrence. Nevertheless, he felt he needed answers to reach closure in his mind about his feelings of unexplained loss. He longed to see his father, talk to him, and ask him questions that plagued his mind. He wanted to know why his father never visited him. He wanted to know if his father ever wanted to be in his life.

Lawrence was reminded of his discomfort about his father missing out on very important occasions in Lawrence's life. The search for answers to these questions produced anxiety feelings in him.

Lawrence demonstrated resentment that the significant people in his life did not help him to meet his father. He verbalized his resentment toward his mother for not providing him with answers to his questions about his father. His feelings were suppressed because his mother had done everything for him except giving him answers to his searching questions. He was also angry at her for doing nothing about his frustration when she was informed by the guidance and counseling office about his plunging grades and the cause for it.

When Lawrence entered college, he concentrated on his studies as a way to cope with his anger and resentment. He accepted his situation by replacing the painful experiences of his childhood with his studies and extracurricular activities. At that stage in his life, he strongly believed that his search for answers was worthwhile and that he was ready to accept whatever outcome resulted from finding his father. Having perceived his independence, Lawrence felt he could make his own decisions without consulting his mother. He invited his father to his twenty-eighth birthday party thrown for him by his girlfriend. When his father arrived at the party, Lawrence was very excited because he found an instant connection with this man whom he had not seen for twenty-three years. He found that he shared similar personality traits with this man. His mother was surprised at Lawrence's excitement, but she was happy for him. She realized how much her son had missed his father, and she felt guilty for not helping him with his search.

He felt that when he was growing up, his mother should have let go of the past events with his father. Instead, she had held on to those experiences and restrained him from meeting his father. He was also confused when his mother did not allow him to visit his uncle, whom he looked up to as a positive role model. Lawrence did not find in his mother's boyfriend a good male role model because he thought the man was taking advantage of his mother's vulnerability. Furthermore, Lawrence experienced rejection from his mother when her boyfriend was present. She gave her total attention to her boyfriend and disregarded

Lawrence. He was also angry with his mother's boyfriend for the continued separation of his parents and his consequent abandonment.

In the face of confusion while searching for his father, Lawrence, by learning from his aunts, became strong and resistant to negative influence. His aunts were strict and instructive, so in the absence of a positive role model, he submitted to their mentoring, which became beneficial for his positive growth and development. Through his aunts he learned problem solving and respectful communication skills. His grandmother was also a strong woman who cared for him and his cousins, so Lawrence was frustrated when his mother did not allow him to stay with his grandmother for the holidays when she asked him to. Through his experience of living with his mother and learning from other female family members, Lawrence became empathetic toward women, a feeling he applied to his wife and his female colleagues.

With his strong Christian upbringing, he was able to maintain a positive self-image. He did not find himself different from his peers who had their fathers in their lives, because his mother, grandmother, and aunts gave him the skills for self-confidence. Though he experienced fatherlessness for most of his life, Lawrence serves as a positive male role model in his family and community. He provides for his family and supports them in positive ways. He also preaches at the local Sunday school in order to bring up children in sound moral environments.

Composite Interpretation of Lawrence's Lived Experience

Confusion. Lawrence was confused about his father's whereabouts for most of his childhood. ("I have known about my father all my life, but I met him for the first time when I was twenty-eight years old.") He knew his father was somewhere out there, so he was confused about why he got no help from anybody to find him. First, his mother forbade him from talking about his father, so he was afraid of hurting her feelings, and he kept his pain to himself. Second, no one was ready to tell him about the cause of his parents' separation. Third, since he had experienced parental love and care until his father left, Lawrence became extremely confused. He lived with his pain until four years later when his mother revealed to him the cause of their divorce, even though she did not give him the details.

He was anxious to meet his father, but he did not know how, so he kept his feelings secret. ("I always had a sincere interest in contacting my father someday, but I was honestly afraid of hurting my mother's feelings.") He longed for answers to why his father, who loved him dearly, would abandon him and his mother without any hint of coming back. ("I am not sure why and when he decided that he would not be part of my life, but my mother single-handedly raised me.")

Since he did not know why his father left, he began to search for him by continually questioning his mother, but his mother refused to talk about his father. ("What I know about my early childhood was that my parents were married before I was born.") This uncertainty made him feel lonely and rejected. ("When Mama began to take me, I asked her why, and she said my dad had left.") He wanted to know where his father was. He was worried whether something bad had happened to him, yet no one was ready to tell Lawrence where he was. ("I asked her so many questions that she got angry and told me not to talk about my father again.")

He began to search for his father in his mind, but he became more confused. ("I kept a lot of pictures of my father in my room. I looked at them each day, but I also longed to see him, talk to him, and ask him questions.") His longing was aggravated by the fact that he was alone in the search for his father, since his mother forbade him to talk about his father. As a result, he demonstrated anxiety, which was a physical manifestation of his confused emotions.

Vulnerability. Lawrence could have contacted his father without his mother knowing about it, but he feared he could not bear the consequences of another rejection from his father. ("I simply did not know how I would deal with the rejection.") This fear arose as a result of not knowing why his father left and why his mother did not want him to know. ("When it became clear to me that my mother did not want me to contact my father, I was wounded and felt unsafe.") As far back as he could remember, Lawrence knew his parents as a married couple. ("What I know about my childhood is that my parents were married before I was born.") During his first four years he enjoyed fatherly love and care until his father left. ("I remember my father driving me to school on my first day, and then, every day.")

Lawrence's fear about his father's sudden desertion was heightened when his mother gave him a blunt, short reply when he asked about the precipitants of his father's leaving. ("She only indicated that they did not get on well and promised to take good care of me.")

In the midst of all these uncertainties, Lawrence feared that without knowing the full answers about his parents' separation, he might live a life in which he would never see his father again. ("I wanted to know if he loved me and if he was willing to be in my life. I wanted to know why he never visited me or attended my basketball games.") Lawrence was afraid, especially when his mother decided to keep him from knowing where his father was and why he abandoned him. ("My mother was informed, but she did not take me to my dad.")

Lawrence's fear was motivated by his anger for not knowing the answers to his questions. ("It became clear to me at that time that I was angry for no apparent reason; my grades had taken a dip, and I thought of dropping out of school.") Consequently, he hardly ever spoke to his mother about his feelings because it was of no use to his goal.

Loneliness. With regard to finding his father, Lawrence thought that his mother's uncompromising behavior was largely due to her boyfriend's presence. "He was always telling her what to do. Mother had no choices, it was always his." His mother would turn her frustrations on Lawrence, asking him to do things her way. He was angry when his mother forbade him to visit his only uncle, who was a pastor. "My uncle always asked my mother to let me visit him when school was on break, but my mother would not let me go." Lawrence felt helpless in the face of not understanding why his mother refused to let him do some of the things he thought were good for him. "But I looked up to my uncle as a positive role model. He advised me to take my studies seriously and always asked me what I wanted to be in the future."

In the absence of his father, and with his mother prohibiting him from visiting his uncle, Lawrence had no male to look up to except his mother's boyfriend. He found the boyfriend, however, to be a bad influence on both himself and his mother. "My mother's boyfriend who lived in our house for a while was not the type I wanted as a role model."

Helplessness. The absence of a loving and caring male role model in his made Lawrence helpless. His mother's insensitivity to his needs became the source of Lawrence's angry feelings. ("She hardly paid attention to me when he was present, so I did not like him. In a way, he was the cause of my mother's hatred for my father.")

Furthermore, he was helpless with his mother's vulnerability that led her boyfriend to take advantage of her. ("My mother never got to do what she wanted to do. Once she wanted to buy a particular car, but her boyfriend dissuaded her into buying something else.") By his mother's own design, however, he could not do anything to help her.

Hurt. Though he acknowledged his mother's immense support to him when he was growing up, Lawrence was angry with her for his father's disappearance. First, he was angry because his mother could not provide him with the answers to his questions about his father. ("I asked her why Dad had stopped taking me to school, and she said my dad had left.") Secondly, he was angry because when she finally decided to give him an answer to his questions, his mother did not give details, leaving him mentally lost. ("She told me she divorced my father because they did not get on well.") His angry feelings were a mask of a deeper emotion of hurt for his loss.

Furthermore, Lawrence was hurt by the presence of his mother's boyfriend, to whom his mother gave all her attention while ignoring him. ("She hardly paid attention to me when he was present, so I did not like him.") He was angry with his mother's boyfriend, who was only there for his selfish motives and whose presence made his mother forbid him from talking about his father. ("My mother's boyfriend was not ready to commit to a relationship because he was not willing to take up the fathering role.") Lawrence believed that mentally his mother was controlled by her boyfriend and that the man did not allow her to do things she wanted. ("These traits seemed to me as though they could turn into mental abuse for my mom.") As he thought about the constant alienation from his mother, he became increasingly hurt because the boyfriend was tearing him and his mother apart by taking full control of his mother's life. It was always the boyfriend's choices that won out. ("My mother never got to do what she wanted to do.")

He was also angry with his father for deserting him very early in his life. He thought that his father did not necessarily need to live with them but could have visited him regularly, as should any father separated from his children's mother. ("But they should endeavor to be physically present for them, play with them, discipline them when they go wrong, and take them to church.")

CHAPTER 4
Perry

I never had a member of my family playing the role of a role model in my life. Honestly, there was no one to look up to or to show me how things were supposed to be done. There was no male role model in my life. I grew up among my mother and my grandmother, and I was raised by both of them. My mother was a single parent. My father left her while she was still pregnant with me, and I have never heard of him nor met him.

I was raised by my mother and my grandmother, both of whom worked full time while I was growing up. My mother was always there for me. I agree that she was sometimes tough on me, but without a male role model to straighten me up, she had to do what she did. Her no-nonsense parenting approach, together with my grandmother's nurturing attitude, molded me to be a strong person. I remember very well when I was in middle school, I was an obedient and respectful kid, coming home from school, letting myself into the apartment that we lived in, starting my homework, and reading, as my mother and grandmother had instructed, before I watched TV. When they came home from work they fixed dinner.

I did not know any of my female family members apart from my mother and my grandmother. My grandmother was like a father to me. She cared for me unconditionally. She seemed to enjoy the companionship, love, and the opportunity to be in my life as a parent. Her main reason for being there for me and my mother was that she saw that we needed her. My grandmother was a wonderful teacher. She taught me to be respectful, humble, and simple in everything that I did.

Even though my mother displayed high levels of physical and emotional control over me, she also showed me warmth and affection and helped to protect me from dangerous neighborhood activities. My mother's parenting style promoted the development of self-regulation in me.

There has not been a day that I did not question my masculinity. I struggle with my manhood. I find it difficult to deal with the ideas and fears at failing in my duties as a protector, leader, the strong yet sensitive one. I have yet to seen myself in action protecting my wife or my children. I depend on other pastors in my church to show me what it means to be masculine. I look up to them in their roles as counselors, loving husbands, and great fathers.

A father's role in bringing up a child is that of a teacher and a moral leader of his family. A father should accept his responsibility of imposing moral standards and promoting his children's rational development. A father should take charge of making childrearing decisions and even assume custody of the children in case of a marital separation. In short, a father should be the strong force in his family and in his community, bringing up his own children in positive ways and helping to bring up others in the community that need positive role models.

Yes, I missed the strong hand of a father that could have guided me to act like a man. I have still not come to terms with my masculinity. Even though I know men have different roles in family life, in practice, I find it difficult to delineate those roles from those of women. I view both roles in the same light. If my father had been in my life, I would have learned to take care of children as a man. I could have understood the strengths and weaknesses of women. My mother was a strong woman, but she lacked the strength of a man—the very strength of character that I needed to stand for my wife and children.

I wanted my father to show me love. Just attending my basketball games and coming for my birthdays meant nothing to me. Those occasions were ordinary social events. He could have been in my life yet be unable to attend my wedding due to sickness or travel. He could not have been there all the time and I could live with it. But he was never there, and the thought of that has affected my psychological frame. Until I am able to feel that I could be loved and accepted by others, my feelings will remain the same.

A positive self-image is what I am struggling to gain. I need to become a man that can protect and lead. A positive self-image would be for me the ability to act with strength yet be sensitive to the feelings and thoughts of others. I have fought with myself for so long for feeling like no one could love me because of the rejection I've felt due to my dad leaving. I pity my wife because she has the burden of dealing with me when I fall into this mindset. Many times, I expect others to give up on me.

As a pastor, I am beginning to learn that it is only through an unconditional love that I can get out of this mindset. But who can give this kind of love except God Almighty? I am not there yet, but I know I will renew my inward-looking self and rid the outer self of its fear. That's my goal. I am a pastor, but I am different from other pastors. It is ridiculous that I am not able to exhibit a sense of benevolent responsibility to lead as a pastor and a father. I am not able to provide for and protect my family and my flock in ways appropriate to a man's differing relationships. I feel physically strong and sexually competent. I am forceful and rational, but I struggle with this immature inner masculinity that makes me hate myself deeply.

Others respect me and see me as a good leader. My sermons and counseling have received the acclaim of both my church and my community. What they don't know is my inner struggles to be a man. I am relieved that I have realized that I am trying to attain that level of manhood that will give me self-confidence and self-belief.

Structural Interpretation of Perry's Lived Experience

Perry's abandonment by his father in his childhood resulted in low self-esteem in his adult life. He acknowledged that apart from his mother and grandmother, he never had a member of his family playing any role in his life. He grew up among his mother and grandmother, both of whom worked full time jobs to take care of him.

The hurt of being abandoned by his father was suppressed by Perry's mother and his grandmother who protected him to cope with life in their difficult neighborhood.

Perry found that his mother's no-nonsense parenting style helped him stay out of drugs and other crimes in the neighborhood. He had to follow a set of rules at homes before he was allowed to watch TV. Perry believed that obeying his mother's rules helped him to stay out of trouble and keep up with his schoolwork.

Perry's grandmother was very active in his life. He called her a good teacher who complemented his mother's tough parenting approach with love and unconditional positive regard. In that way, Perry was able to learn to be trustful rather than resentful.

Perry assumed that his grandmother taught him to be respectful, obedient, and humble. He felt a need, however, for a male type of parenting to make him complete as a man, so he kept searching for this much-needed unconditional acceptance, validation, and love of a father. As a result of this unmet childhood developmental need, Perry struggled to take care of his children as a father.

Additionally, Perry believed that being raised totally by women made him struggle on different occasions to deal with his role as a father and mentor in his community. He depended on his colleagues to be able to carry on his duties as a pastor. Perry was confused about the roles of men compared to those of women in family life. He knew those roles but in practice, he struggled to delineate them to educate, counsel, and lead others in his family, church, and community. This shortfall resulted in low self-esteem when it came to performing his duties as a pastor in which he was faced with teaching and counseling others and helping them make important life decisions.

Perry showed that he struggled with making decisions and undertaking independent tasks at home and in his church. When it came to standing up for his family, Perry found it difficult to act as the head of the household. His wife had to step in whenever Perry fell into that mindset. He also exhibited a tendency to read too much into things; this made it difficult for his wife to respond to him because she felt that she was doing something wrong to him.

Perry's lack of strength in the face of challenges was a source of pain to him, and he looked up to his senior pastors and elders to give him guidance. He believed that since he did not receive love from his father, others were going to reject him as well. Before he gave a sermon to his church members, he struggled with removing that sense of rejection so as to be able to speak like a pastor. He felt strong in other areas of his life, but his struggle with the immature inner masculinity made him hate himself.

Composite Interpretation of Perry's Lived Experience

Shame. Perry was ashamed that because of the abandonment he faced in his childhood, he was not able to perform his duties as a father and a pastor. ("It is ridiculous that I am not able to exhibit a sense of benevolent responsibility to lead as a pastor and a father.") ("I never had a member of my family playing the role of a role model in my life.")

Perry grieved as he went through the shameful experience of living through his childhood without support from his father who deserted him when his mother was pregnant. ("My father left while she was pregnant with me, and I have never met nor seen him again.") He felt that he might have done something wrong or his mother did something wrong that made his father not ever show up in his life. ("He could not have been there all the time and I could live with it. But he was never there, and the thought of that has affected my psychological frame.")

His fear of his abandonment was increased by the fact that there was no other person apart from his mother and grandmother in his life. ("Honestly, there was no one to look up to or to show me how things were supposed to be done.") His mother had a no-nonsense parenting approach. ("I agree that she was sometimes tough on me, but without a male role model to straighten me up, she had to do what she did.") Perry also described his grandmother as being like a father to him. Though he felt protected by his mother and grandmother from the neighborhood activities in his childhood, Perry was ashamed of his peerless childhood that made him isolated in his neighborhood and impacted his adult life. ("Yes, I missed the strong hand of a father that could have guided me to act like a man.")

Perry was traumatized by the loss of his father in his childhood, but as he was not allowed to grieve it, he grew up carrying the shame of it into his adulthood, which in turn caused him a lot of pain. ("There has not been a day that I did not question my masculinity. I struggle with my manhood.")

Hurt. Perry blamed his lack of masculinity—which impacted his ability to protect his family, lead his church members, and mentor in his community—on the effects of his abandonment. ("The role of a father is that of a teacher and a moral leader of his family. A father should accept his responsibility of imposing moral standards and promoting his children's rational development.") But he worried whether his own childhood issues had prevented him from attaining that level of strength to perform his duties as a father. ("I have still not come to terms with my masculinity.")

Having been abandoned by his father in his childhood, Perry feared that he might be abandoned by the people around him, so he found it difficult to trust others. ("Until I am able to feel that I could be loved and accepted by others, my feelings will remain the same.") ("I pity my wife because she has the burden of dealing with me when I fall into this mindset. Many times, I expect others to give up on me.")

Perry was angry with his father for not being in his life; deep inside him was a pervasive hurt that he had not learned to own and express appropriately. ("But he was never there, and the thought of that has affected my psychological frame.")

Perry was hurt for not being strong enough to care for his family. ("I am not able to exhibit a sense of benevolent responsibility to lead, provide for, and protect my family and my flock in ways appropriate to a man's differing relationships.") His struggle to take up his manly role was a source of frustration and anger to him, but he was actually hurt for his inability to act like other men. ("I am relieved that I am trying to attain that level of manhood that will give me self-confidence and self-belief.")

Vulnerability. Perry was angry with his father for abandoning him, but a closer analysis of his emotions revealed that his anger was a mask for his feelings of being vulnerable. ("I have fought with myself for so long for feeling like no one could love me because of the rejection I've felt due to my dad leaving.") ("As a pastor, I am beginning to learn that it is only through an unconditional love that I can get out of this mindset.")

He was also angry that his father's absence in his life caused him to be disconnected with the outside world. This disconnection made him feel vulnerable and thought that he was not capable of discharging his duties as a husband and father. ("If my father had been in my life, I would have learned to take care of children as a man.")

Additionally, Perry felt that living in a fatherless home had affected his ability to act with confidence. ("A positive self-image would be for me the ability to act with strength yet be sensitive to the feelings and thoughts of others.") His fear of social situations was caused by his father's desertion. ("I am not there yet, but I know I will renew the inward-looking self and rid the outer self of its fear.") Perry believed that he possessed wonderful traits and attributes but that these were overshadowed by his lack of confidence which was driven by his fear of rejection. ("I am forceful and rational, but I struggle with this immature inner masculinity that makes me hate myself deeply.")

He also demonstrated a fear of failure because ever since his childhood, he never trusted himself at succeeding at tasks. ("I find it difficult to deal with the ideas and fears at failing in my duties as a protector, leader, the strong yet sensitive one.") ("What they don't know is my inner struggles to be a man.")

Confusion. With his continued search for answers regarding his abandonment, Perry sought help from God, whom he believed had answers to everyone's questions. ("But who can give this kind of love except God Almighty.") Having been raised by his mother and grandmother, Perry was confused with the role of a father in family life. ("Even though I know men have different roles in family life, in practice, I find it difficult to delineate those roles from those of women; I view both roles in the same light.")

Even though he appreciated the efforts of his mother and grandmother in his upbringing, he was confused as to why his mother and grandmother refused to tell him about his father. He conjectured that they tried hard to stand in for his father, but he believed he needed a male in his life to guide him. ("I was raised by my mother and grandmother, both of whom worked full time while I was growing up.") ("A father should take charge of making childrearing decisions and even assume custody of the children in case of a marital separation; in short, a father should be the strong force in his family and in his community, bringing up his own children in positive ways and helping to bring up others in the community.")

Not knowing the circumstances that caused his abandonment, Perry felt uncertain about the world around him, and this was a source of fear for him. ("Many times, I expect others to give up on me.") He was confused and unable to act correctly in his duties. ("I find it difficult to deal with ideas and fears of failing in my duties as a protector, leader, and the strong yet sensitive one.")

He could hardly understand whose fault it was that he grew up without his father. ("But he was never there, and the thought of that has affected my psychological frame.")

CHAPTER 5
Dontae

There are many things I would like to say about my childhood, but I don't know where to begin. Sometimes I feel like I should not think about the fact that I don't know who my father is. It is painful, and by allowing the thoughts to surface, I relive the emotional trauma of growing up in total poverty, being left with countless strangers while my mother worked as a waitress to barely feed me and my sisters.

I was the youngest of my mother's three children. My two sisters were older than me, but they also did not know who our father was, so I erroneously concluded that we had different fathers. My mother did not talk about our father; she only called him names such as "deadbeat," "hopeless man," and "a junkie." Even to this day we have not seen this man.

My mother had a brother, but he was an alcoholic. He never came home unless he was drunk and needed food to eat. It was horrible. He would come and eat what my mother had struggled to provide us as she continued to work as a waitress.

As for my grandfather, he took me out to fish. He disciplined me, but he also cared for me. He was my friend because he was the only person who understood my struggles with my thoughts. Grandpa talked to me about education and church.

My mother was always in our lives. My grandmother was not that physically strong but when we had nothing to eat she gave us what she had. My aunts were lightly involved in my life, but we were not geographically close to them.

I see women differently; it depends on how they approach me. Initially, I felt women determined my life. I respect them for that. I feel they need the help and companionship of their partners to bring out their potential. I provided for my wife and now she is self-sufficient. She respects and trusts me. Growing up, my mother left me in the care of different neighbors each time she went to work. Each day, I experienced the care of a different woman. Some of these experiences were good, but most of the time I felt lonely and abused. There was one woman who would give me food to eat even when my mother had not returned from her job. However, some of the women waited for my mother to return, but others left me out while they served lunch and dinner to their children. The rest made me work—wash and clean—before giving me food to eat. These are the experiences that shaped my views about women.

Fathers should be the livewire of their children. From my experience, I believe that the presence or absence of a father in a child's life determines who or what the child will grow up to be in the future. They are the important connection to children and their behavior. Even if a father is poor, he should be present in his children's lives. Fathers should be there to teach and direct their children. My grandmother had to connect me to my first girlfriend, who eventually became my wife, because I was too shy to approach females when I was in high school.

A child without a father is like a lost sheep. Up till now, I fear wide open spaces because I feel lost in them. I believe that my father should have loved me enough to play a part in my life. He should have realized that I represent his body and that he should have helped me to become my own person through his guidance. Yes. There were many opportunities that I missed because I had no father. I believe his absence changed my destiny. I cannot forget having no one to fall on in those times of difficulties. I felt lost many times. When I asked my mother for things and she could not afford them, there was no other person to fall on. My grandparents had grown old and could hardly support themselves. These are experiences I have to work hard to forget. They gave me a kick in the gut, lowered my self-esteem, and made me feel worthless.

The damage of my childhood experiences has formed my personality and affected the way I feel inside. I wonder what changes can take place to remove the core of my being.

With senses of respect, responsibility, and confidence one can be successful in life. My father's alienation has caused me to believe that I cannot have my way in life. I do not take anything for granted. I need to struggle very hard to get anything I want in life. I am different in many ways.

At my age, I feel I am too shy to attend social functions. This was my life story until I entered Bible college to learn to become a pastor. Even with my training of speaking in public places I find it difficult to make eye contact. I hide these feelings when I face a large audience. Before a large audience, I don't feel the stare of an individual; I speak to my audience like to a wall. I am weird.

I think those kids with their fathers are lucky. They are able to identify their unique qualities. I grew up most of time not knowing who I was. I was not sure what next was going to happen to me. I did not know where my next meal was coming from. My poor mother struggled hard to get food for us. We spent Christmas and Thanksgiving alone without gifts or special meals. I remember when I was in high school, a friend of mine brought a piece of the turkey meal his family had at Thanksgiving to school the next day for me.

My humility, self-respect, and listening skills have placed me in a leadership position in my community. I wonder if others feel my pain. I don't think they do, because no one has talked to me about my shyness or my lack of assertiveness. They don't question why I don't engage in social activities. I believe in myself, but I don't know if others believe in me.

Structural Interpretation of Dontae's Lived Experience

Dontae suffered from emotional pain throughout his life as a consequence of not knowing who his father was. Additionally, because of poverty his life was devoid of a stable social network or warm, close bonds. He became aware of the pain and suffering of his childhood through what was happening in his adult life. Whenever he thought about the possibility that his father chose to abandon him willingly, he became increasingly afraid. As a result of his father's deliberate desertion, Dontae's mother had to work as a waitress to take care of him and his sisters.

The memory of these past experiences seemed to move along with his life. Dontae's memory was clogged with the wound of not knowing who his father was, which he felt kept happening to him. Whenever he re-experienced what happened in his formative years, Dontae became confused. Because he was conditioned by his pain, he found it difficult to move on without bringing along the memory of his childhood rejection. When he looked around for a father figure, he found none, especially when his mother's brother, who could have served in that role, was an alcoholic who depended on his mother's meager income. Dontae believed that his life was blocked on all sides by loneliness.

To add to his pain, Dontae's mother had to leave him with different neighbors all the time. His care was in the hands of many different people who were forced to watch him. With strangers taking care of him, Donate did not experience the love that a child needed to develop appropriately. As a result of experiencing various levels of caregiving from women in his neighborhood, he felt alienated most of the time. Consequently, each of these levels of caregiving influenced his mindset about how to deal with women. Additionally, Dontae experienced extreme loneliness when his mother left him in the care of strange women. When he would recall those moments of loneliness and rejection, Dontae became confused and distressed. These stressful experiences led to his resistance to involvement in social situations because of his fear of doing something embarrassing front of others.

Composite Interpretation of Dontae's Lived Experience

Shame. Dontae's development was marked with a lot of painful experiences. ("I relive the emotional trauma of growing up in total poverty.") He had sad memories of how, without his father, his mother had to go through much hardship to bring him and his sisters up in poor conditions. ("From my experience, I believe that the presence or absence of a father in a child's life determines who or what the child will grow up to be in the future.")

Dontae found it uncomfortable and disempowering to express his shame of his experiences, so he demonstrated grief instead. ("I did not know where my next meal was coming from. I was not sure what was going to happen to me next.")

He could not openly express his shame of living in poverty during his childhood, yet each day he was reminded about those traumatic experiences as he went through his work as a pastor. ("It is painful and

I do not want these thoughts to surface.") ("These are experiences I have to work hard to forget.")

He was also ashamed of being left in the care of different caregivers as his mother went to work. ("Each day I experienced the care of a different woman.") His experiences with these caregivers provided him with a spontaneous understanding of the struggles of his formative years. ("Some of these experiences were good, but most of the time, I felt lonely and abused.")

Dontae struggled to verbalize the painful aspects of the experiences he faced during his childhood because he felt they were embarrassing and hurtful. ("There are things I would like to say about my childhood, but I don't know where to begin.")

During the years of being defined by his abandonment, he grieved the loss of his father, even though hid his feelings under the mask of passivity about the experience. ("Sometimes I feel I should not think about the fact that I don't know who my father is.") When he looked back to the days his mother had to work hard to take care of him and his sisters, the times that he could not get food to eat, the times that he did not get the privilege of gifts at Thanksgiving and Christmas, and a particular time when he relied on his friend's Thanksgiving leftovers as his celebratory meal, Dontae felt ashamed. ("It is painful, and by allowing the thoughts to surface, I relive the emotional trauma of growing up in total poverty.")

He survived, but the emotional marks those experiences left on his mind influenced his future life.

Vulnerability. Dontae's fears were daily confirmed when he had to be left in the care of someone to whom he was not emotionally attached. Dontae feared that he was going to be abandoned again each time his mother had to leave him with other people. ("Each day, I experienced the care of a different woman.") The effects of these experiences produced anxious feelings in Dontae. ("Some of these experiences were good, but most of the time, I felt lonely and abused.")

He kept these experiences to himself, along with their emotional effects. He feared that he might face rejection if he talked about the negative experiences. ("The damage of my childhood experiences has formed my personality and affected the way I feel inside.") Since he did not talk about them, he could not manage them appropriately, nor could his mother recognize or acknowledge his feelings about them. Consequently, he carried the effects of his feelings alone. ("I wonder what changes can take place to remove the core of my being.")

His greatest fear was that he might never know his father, because his older sisters also did not know about their father or whether they had the same father. ("My sisters were older than me, but they also did not know who our father was, so I concluded that we had different fathers.")

He feared that the need to feel that he was secure and being cared for by someone who is bigger and in control was not provided in his case. ("My mother had a brother, but he was an alcoholic. He never came home unless he was drunk and needed food to eat. It was horrible.") The lack of control and security created uncertainty in his mind. ("Fathers should be the livewire of their children; they are the important connection to children and their behavior.")

Loneliness. Without a father, and with his mother out all day working, Dontae was alone throughout his childhood. The loneliness that Dontae encountered led to anxiety. ("I relive the emotional trauma of growing up in total poverty, being left with countless strangers while my mother worked as a waitress to barely feed me and my sisters.")

In his loneliness, Dontae realized that it was difficult for those around him to recognize his feelings of abandonment, so he kept his emotions to himself. ("The damage of my childhood experiences has formed my personality and affected the way I feel inside.") He kept his feelings of hurt and anxiety inside.

Dontae was anxious of the fact that when he was in need there was no one to fall on. ("When I asked my mother for things and she could not afford them, there was no other person to fall on.") These anxious feelings were engendered by a deeper emotion of helplessness that he harbored during his childhood days. ("However, some of the women waited for my mother to return, but others left me out while they served lunch and dinner to their children. The rest made me work—wash and clean—before giving me food to eat.") This cycle of his anxiety was triggered by his abandonment experiences that made him helpless, leading to a feeling of insecurity in later years. ("A child without a father is like a lost sheep … I felt lost many times.") ("I don't take anything for granted.")

As he grew up, he continued to be vigilant and ready for action, which reflected his cognitive state of relative helplessness. ("These are experiences I have to work hard to forget. They gave me a kick in the gut, lowered my self-esteem, and made me feel worthless.")

Confusion. Dontae's experience of growing up without a father led to feelings of worthlessness and low self-esteem. ("I have fought with myself for so long for feeling like no one could love me because of the rejection I've felt due to my dad leaving.") With a father, Dontae said, ("one can be successful in life and gain respect, be responsible, and have confidence.") Without one, he felt worthless and vulnerable. ("There were many opportunities that I missed because I had no father.")

He referred to his father's absence as a basis for his psychological mindset. ("His alienation has caused me to believe that I cannot have my way in life. I need to struggle very hard to get anything I want in life.") At the age of 48, Dontae still felt shy in social encounters. He struggled to accept the compliments of his congregation and peers, and he did not feel accepted in his own family. ("I am too shy to attend social functions.") As a pastor, an important part of his duties was to give sermons to large audiences, but sometimes he found it difficult to carry out this important function because of how he felt about himself. ("Even with my training of speaking in public places, I find it difficult to make eye contact.")

He could not acknowledge the existence of his fear because he underestimated the power he had to do so. Rather, he held on to his childhood wounds and remained confused. ("I wonder if others feel my pain. I don't think they do, because no one has talked about my shyness or my lack of assertiveness.") Whenever he was to face an audience, he assumed he was not going to do well, so he went on to imagine that others would see through his grief. ("The damage of my childhood experiences has formed my personality and affected the way I feel inside.") He grew up thinking that his experiences were unusual, so he felt vulnerable as he lived in fear that someone would find out. ("I wonder what changes can take place to remove the core of my being.")

Worthlessness. Growing up without knowing who his father was, Dontae felt that he lost every good thing in his childhood. ("Sometimes I feel like I should not think about the fact that I don't know who my father is.") His mother, who was the closest person in his life, was not there most of the time, because she had to work each day to feed him and his sisters. ("I relive the emotional trauma of growing up in total poverty, being left with countless strangers while my mother worked as a waitress to barely feed me and my sisters.")

Dontae underrated his capabilities because he felt worthless in the face of stress. ("At my age, I feel I am too shy to attend social functions.") His sense of loss was increased with the memory of the many different caregivers with whom his mother left him and who were changed each day and were strangers with whom he had no attachment. ("Each day, I experienced the care of a different woman.")

One person in Dontae's life who could have had a positive influence on him was his mother's only brother. But he lost him to alcohol addiction. ("My mother had a brother but he was an alcoholic.") Looking at his uncle's worthless nature, Dontae became anxious for fear of becoming like his uncle. ("He never came home unless he was drunk and needed food to eat; it was horrible.") Having been abandoned by his father, Dontae grieved the loss of a positive male role model who could have taught him how to appreciate himself and learn new things. ("I think those kids with their fathers are lucky.")

Dontae felt he lost the opportunities his father could have given him if he were in his life. ("There were many opportunities that I missed because I had no father.") He strongly believed that he could have been someone better if he had not been abandoned by his father. ("I believe his absence changed my destiny.") He acknowledged that his mother and grandmother were always there for him, but he missed the guidance and support of a male figure to be able to do the things men do. ("My grandmother had to connect me to my girlfriend, who eventually became my wife, because I was shy to approach females when I was in high school.") These influences were created by the losses he had faced in the past that made him feel anxious all through his life. ("These are experiences I have to work hard to forget. They gave me a kick in the gut, lowered my self-esteem and made me feel worthless.")

CHAPTER 6
Peter

I don't know if I should say that I had a good childhood. I was born into a large Christian family in which my grandmother was the head. There were males living there too, but Grandma was the boss. My mother, aunts, and cousins lived there too.

My mother was a beautiful woman, but she made a lot of wrong choices. As far as I can remember, she never worked, so she could not cater for our needs—me and my two sisters. She was always drinking and smoking and she had a lot of male friends, some of whom came to sleep in our room at night. It was horrible. Momma would kick us out of the room when she brought a man home, and she did so many times. But I loved my mother, and I wished she could change and put her body down for us.

The behaviors of my aunts were not different from my mother's. They drank and made loud noise at night when they came home from the club. They were up to no good. Not even one of them. They just kept having kids with no dads.

Grandma would take us in, especially during the cold season. As for Grandma, she was always talking. She would advise us to be good kids and not follow our mother's habits. On Sundays, Grandma would take us to church—me, my sisters, and my cousins. My mother, aunts, and uncles never went to church.

I do not know my father till this day. My grandmother told me that no one owned up as my biological father. My mother did not know who he was. Maybe she knew but she was ashamed to say it. But I understand.

Most of Momma's men friends were drug addicts and alcoholics. Momma herself was always drunk. One night a man gave me a cigarette to smoke. My mother did not stop him, but thanks to my grandmother, I ran to her and she came in to kick the man out of our house. My mother was not much in my life; she was busy with her own life. Most of my uncles who lived in our house drank and smoked. I did not see their wives, but they had girlfriends who had children too.

My grandmother believed that I was not safe in the neighborhood because most of the males were drug addicts and dealers. She ensured that I understood the negative effects of substance use. She told me to be careful with whatever I put into my body. Grandma showed me how to be compassionate and respectful to others. She also took care of the children my aunts and uncles brought home. She gave them food and a place to sleep. But as much as she tried, some of my cousins turned to drugs and alcohol. There were no positive male role models in the family.

When I was eight years old, Grandma called me into her room and told me, "You and your sisters are not safe in this neighborhood." So she wanted to send me out of there before I joined those "junkies." She sent me to the city to live with my uncle. My uncle who lived in the city did not drink nor smoke. He made sure that I joined his family at church on Sundays. He also ensured that I went to school. My uncle's wife took good care of me. She gave me what I lost in my mother—nurturing. I was really happy in my uncle's house. My uncle was a strict disciplinarian. He taught me how to speak with respect and not to curse, and his wife taught me to be respectful to women. These were the two positive attributes that I brought into my married life. I respect my wife and show empathy to other people, especially females. When there was a problem, I was always ready to compromise and bring a solution.

I don't know about how fathers should bring up their children. Maybe, it is because my own father did not play any part in bringing me up. Sometimes, I think that if my father had been in my life, he wouldn't have been a better parent. In fact, I am angry about the whole father situation, but I equally blame my mother for not being there for me and my sisters. I have forgiven whoever my father was, since I do not know him. I wish he could own up and identify himself with me. In that way, I could get some closure and move on with my life. I cared less about him missing out on the major transitions in my life, because my uncle was there all the time.

Fathers should care for their children and be there for them. My uncle was a good father. He attended all of our church activities. He was always at my cousin's basketball games. I could talk to him and he would answer me. He was an example of what the Bible tells us about God, our Heavenly Father. He corrected you when you went wrong and praised you for a good job done.

I substituted the thought of my parents being absent in my life with the pleasantness of living comfortably with my uncle, his wife and children. The thought of them being there for me helped me to manage my anger toward my parents in positive ways.

As I said, I don't care about the absence of my father in my life. I have never for once stopped to consciously reflect on my experiences. My experience in my uncle's house helped me to take life for granted. Up till now, my uncle has been my role model; whatever I am now, and however I carry myself, was made possible by my uncle.

To me, a positive self-image is being confident and owning up to one's responsibilities. I bring up my children in Christian principles that teach them to be respectful and considerate in their dealings with others. The ability to show respect and empathy to others projects one as a courageous and principled human being.

In many ways, I look different from my peers, because I feel unimportant and worthless on certain occasions. Therefore, I approach things with caution so that I don't fail. My wife calls it my fear of rejection, but I think it is a fear of failure. My childhood developed like it was a contract with my grandmother and my uncle. That is, I should not fail them like my other cousins who took to drugs did. I am proactive in making decisions. I hardly go to social functions such as parties and clubs. This does not mean I am an antisocial creature. Rather, I am meditative. I prefer to be away from the hustle and bustle of social places. I feel safe with my wife by my side. I always need someone who loves me, accepts me, and is ready to protect me. She served as my trusted confidant when it came to finances, my looks, how I treated others, and how I treated myself. I need her to remind me of very little things.

My wife thinks I am a loving and caring person. My children believe in me and think that I am honest with them in every way. That is how others see me too. My colleagues would describe me as a lucky person who made good use of the opportunities that my uncle and my grandmother provided me.

Life is what you make of it. I always pray that I should be mindful of my obligations to others.

Structural Interpretation of Peter's Lived Experience

As a child Peter seemed vulnerable, so he felt anxious most of his childhood. Peter was searching for compensating strategies to deal with being abandoned by his father, thus his grandmother's intervention lessened the pain of feeling on edge most of the time. He was angry when his mother brought different men to the house. He felt lonely and rejected because he did not understand why his mother could kick him and his two sisters from their room so that she could sleep with men there.

With a strong Christian belief imbued in him by his grandmother, Peter was able to cope with his anxiety when he went to live with his uncle. The change of environment was a positive direction that molded Peter's future life and turned around his painful childhood experiences of living with the inherent risks of parental negligence and substance abuse. Perceiving the recurrent drug and alcohol use in his family, Peter was afraid that he risked continuing the intergenerational cycle himself. Many of his male cousins in the neighborhood turned to drugs and alcohol, while the females turned to prostitution. Therefore, he was relieved to be taken out of the environment, because it eased his worry and fear. Peter was not only worried about his mother due to her behaviors; he was also worried about his sisters because losing them in addition to his father would have been devastating for him.

He derived his humble and cautious nature from his grandmother, whom he did not want to fail. Though Peter forgave his father for abandoning him, he still felt angry for the irresponsible parenting situation in which he grew up.

Composite Interpretation of Peter's Lived Experience

Confusion. Peter was hesitant when he began to tell the story of his childhood experiences. Looking back at those experiences, he was surprised at how his mother, aunts and cousins indulged in negative behaviors. ("It was horrible.") Peter was confused with his upbringing, which was a combination of his grandmother's concern and his mother's indifference. ("I don't know if I should say I had a good childhood.") Peter was also confused with the activities that went on during his formative years, especially the people he found himself with, so he sought to bring meaning to it. ("I was born into large Christian family in which my grandmother was the head.")

He wondered why his mother, a very beautiful woman, was drinking and prostituting. ("My mother was a beautiful woman, but she made wrong choices. As far as I can remember, she never worked, so she could not cater for our needs—me and my two sisters.")

He was worried about the behaviors of his family members that ran counter to the beliefs and practices of his grandmother. ("My mother, aunts, and uncles never went to church.") The men in his family used drugs. Peter said that "most of my uncles who lived in our house drank and smoked," while the females were prostituting. ("The behaviors of my aunts were not different from my mother's.")

In addition to the confusion surrounding his father's desertion, Peter bore the pain of the neglect he lived through as a result of his mother's behavior. ("My mother was not much in my life; she was busy with her own life.") He remembered his mother bringing home different men each night and asking him and his sisters to quit the room although they did not know where they were going to sleep. Peter was angry when he relived these moments. ("Momma would kick us out of the room when she brought a man home, and she did so many times.")

When he remembered the uncertainty that his mother's behavior created for him and his sisters, Peter became angry. Though he loved his mother ("but I loved my mother") he was afraid of the unpredictability of her actions. ("And I wished she could change and put her body down for us.") His mother's actions confounded him, so he wondered how his life would have been if his father had not abandoned him. ("Sometimes, I think that if my father had been in my life, he wouldn't have done better.") At this stage, Peter was not so much worried about being abandoned by his father as he was about his mother drinking and prostituting.

Vulnerability. Peter was afraid for his mother when he left her behind for his uncle's house, departing the home of his grandmother. ("She would advise us to be good kids and not follow our mother's habits.") He feared that his mother would face the negative consequences of her habitual drinking and prostituting. ("Most of Momma's men friends were drug addicts and alcoholics. Momma herself was always drunk.")

He lived with the hurtful feelings of abandonment, but he was silent about them because he was afraid he might encounter additional alienation. ("I do not know my father till this day. My grandmother told me no one owned up as my biological father. My mother did not know who he was. Maybe she knew, but she was ashamed to say it. But I understand.") He was cautious as he lived in his uncle's house for fear that he might be kicked out if he misbehaved.

When Peter indicated that ("in many ways, I look different from my peers, because I approach things with caution,") he was actually afraid of failing at his uncle's house. ("My wife calls it the fear of the unknown, but I think it is a fear of failure.") His fear was driven by the thought that he was spatially and temporally safe from the dangers of his early childhood experiences, and therefore, he was afraid of failing his grandmother. ("My childhood developed like it was a contract with my grandmother and my uncle. That is, I should not fail them like my other cousins who took drugs did.")

Loneliness. Growing up as a child in his family house, Peter felt lonely all the time. His loneliness was masked by his feelings of anxiety and uncertainty. ("I don't know if I should say I had a good childhood.") His anxiety stemmed from the activities of his mother and aunts that were counterproductive for his development. ("They drank and made loud noise at night when they came home from the club.")

As he grieved his abandonment by his father, he worried about losing his mother because she was never there for him. ("My mother was not much in my life; she was busy with her own life.")

Peter questioned the loss of a positive role model who could have directed and instructed his family members to live responsibly. ("I think there was a need for positive male role models in the family.") He believed that his mother and aunts were leading destructive lives and the only way to save them was to get someone who could straighten them up. Unfortunately, his uncles were themselves bad influences on the women and children. ("Most of my uncles who lived in our house drank and smoked.")

All these experiences created a sense of loss in Peter that he masked with anger. ("I am angry about the whole father situation, but I equally blame my mother for not being there for me and my sisters.") Since there were no avenues to express his sense of loss, he responded to his invisible injuries by hiding them below the surface of his pain.

Worthlessness. Peter described leading a life of caution, which was the result of the anxiety that had decreased his self-esteem. ("In many ways, I feel different from my peers, because I feel unimportant and worthless on certain occasions. Therefore, I approach things with caution so that I don't fail.") His cautious actions were defined by his lack of self-confidence that affected his social and other areas of his adult life. ("I hardly go to social functions such as parties and clubs. This does not mean I am an antisocial creature. Rather, I am meditative. I prefer to be away from the hustle and bustle of the social places.") He showed that he needed to be reassured into making important decisions. ("My finances, my looks, how I treat others, and how I treat myself. Someone needs to remind me.")

Peter's feelings of worthlessness and inadequacy were a mask for the absence of security in his childhood. ("I feel safe with my wife by my side. I always need someone who loves me, accepts me, and is ready to protect me.") Without the protection he received from his grandmother during his childhood and the safety of his uncle's home, Peter now depended on individuals such as his wife to provide him those supports.

CHAPTER 7
Frederick

I was separated from my mother when I was a baby because she was a teenager. I never knew who my father was. My grandparents raised me from babyhood until I was five years old. My grandparents were good to me and took care of me. One day, my mother visited and complained to them about my weight. Instead of staying to take good care of me, she blamed them for being bad parents, so when she left my grandparents deserted me. The rest of my childhood and adolescence was tough.

I was homeless, so I lived in the streets at the mercy of rapists and drug sellers. I was beaten and sexually abused and I spent most of the time hungry and cold.

At one point, I met my mother because she went to look for me at my grandparents' house and was told I had run away. She gave me some money but she went away. That was the last time I saw her.

One day, as I was sleeping on the curb, a man took me home and asked his wife to take good care of me. They taught me to read and write and also taught me carpentry.

At a point, they too abandoned me, so I took to the streets again, but this time I sold drugs. When I was eighteen years old, I was arrested for selling cocaine and thrown into jail. I continued to sell drugs in prison because I could bribe some prison officers who helped me to receive marijuana from outside the jailhouse to sell to fellow inmates, but when I was caught, my jail term was increased. As I came out, drug peddling was all I could do. It was good business at first, but when one of my boys was murdered, I decided to quit.

The Good Samaritan who found me in the streets had been my male role model at first. He and his wife taught me a lot of good things. But just like my grandparents abandoned me at the age of five years for doing nothing wrong, he also asked me to leave for no reason. I hated them. I don't know any other male family member who has been in my life.

My grandmother was a kind person. She acted like my mother and my father, but she also listened to her husband and kicked me out of their house.

I hardly saw my mother and so I did not know her siblings. I don't know if I have aunts and uncles. It seemed I was alone in this world. I hated them all. My mother, my grandparents, and the Good Samaritan let me down. Family members did not play any role in my life.

I struggled very hard in the cold gutters. I see the world as an unfriendly place. You have to carry your own burden because no one will carry it for you.

Fathers should be involved in their children's upbringing. If my father was supportive, I would have been to school. It would not have taken me twenty-eight years before I got my GED.

I think about how I do not get along with my peers. I have been fighting and swearing all the time. My father could have helped me to adjust to different experiences. There was no one to guide me. It was my entire fault. I don't even have a friend who has completed college. All my buddies are in the streets. I wished someone had saved my life when I was in the streets. I could have been someone different.

My father and everyone else messed my life up. I did not know him, so how could I know how he would have treated me. Maybe he would have done the same things the others did—abandon me. I don't care about him. When I needed him he was not there. I don't know how he looks like. My mother or my grandparents could have done me a favor by showing me his picture. I would go and look for him and tell him my piece of mind. He has destroyed my life. I did not come to this world on my own—they brought me here and they think it was all a joke. They can go to hell. It is hard for me to forgive and forget. That affects my relationships with others. I am afraid that the relationships I have will fail.

Whenever someone comes into my life and shows me love, I think they are pretending and may have some ulterior motives. I think I don't love myself. I have a few friends whose fathers were in their lives because they paid child support for their upkeep. I had nothing like that. My mother and my grandparents used it for themselves if it was paid to them. I don't trust any of them.

I am sorry for my girlfriend. She loves me, and she is faithful to me. But I always accused her of cheating on me. She got pregnant once, but we had to abort it because I continually accused her of cheating. My friends see me as an angry man, but I do not understand why I cannot control my anger. If it goes to the extreme, I fight and hurt people.

Structural Interpretation of Frederick's Lived Experience

Frederick's childhood was interspersed with experiences of separation and abandonment as a result of the effects of teenage motherhood. He felt his parents were unskilled when he was brought forth, so he was angry with both of them. In addition to Frederick's pain of being born to teenage parents, his father ran away, leaving the burden of caregiving to his mother, who was unfit at the time to take care of him. His grandparents took care of Frederick, hoping that his mother would continue with her schooling. Instead, Frederick's mother went back to the streets to continue with a promiscuous life. This infuriated Frederick's grandparents, so they threw him into the streets to find his mother and fend for himself. They were angry because Frederick's mother did not obey their instructions. They threw him out so that Fredrick's mother would take up her responsibilities as a mother.

His search for his mother resulted in all kinds of hardship including homelessness, physical and sexual abuse, and hunger. His pain was compounded when he found his mother, who only gave him some money and sent him back to the streets.

His continued search for his father led him to a stranger who took him to his home and family to care for Frederick but who also threw him back into the streets. These unexplained losses and rejection were sources of anger and confusion for Frederick. As he had nowhere else to go, Frederick joined gangs who sold drugs, and at that young age, he made a lot of money.

Life in the streets had made him impulsive and affected his ability to control risky behaviors. Again, he faced alienation when he was arrested and sent to jail at the age of 18. In prison, he continued searching for attachment figures, and when he was released, Frederick continued to sell drugs. His risk-taking behavior created feelings of rebellion, aggression, rage, and self-destructiveness. He only quit when he was faced with imminent death.

Frederick did not experience the involvement of individuals who loved him in his life. As a result, he felt lost, so he continued to search for acceptance, love, shelter, and nurturing from anyone who could provide them to him. He coped with his rejection by selling and using drugs, and as he continued to face desertion from significant individuals in his life, he found it difficult to give up these habits. He resented his mother and father for abandoning him very early in life. His feelings of rejection and abandonment were increased because he was unable to make a conscious choice to forget the past and get on with his life. He was full of hate for all the people around him. He felt he was misunderstood by those who were close to him. He hated his grandparents for sending him to the streets at a young age. He felt betrayed by individuals who were supposed to care for him. He resented the "Good Samaritan" who saved him from the harshness of the streets but dumped him back there later on.

He did not trust anyone because he felt that the reason for being abandoned by others was that he was not important to his family, friends, and every other person. The anger and mistrust that built up in his mind resulted in Frederick not getting along well with his peers, and he repeatedly accused his girlfriend of cheating.

Composite Interpretation of Frederick's Lived Experience

Confusion. Frederick was angry most of his childhood because he faced abandonment very early in his life. ("My friends see me as an angry man, but I do not understand why I cannot control my anger.") His confusion emanated from how he was separated from his mother immediately after he was born. ("I was separated from my mother when I was a baby.") His grandparents who took care of him also abandoned him after his mother had an altercation with his grandparents about the way he was being raised. ("One day, my mother visited and complained to them about my weight. Instead of staying to take good care of me, she blamed them for being bad parents, so when she left my grandparents deserted me. The rest of my childhood and adolescence was tough.")

He was confused because at an early age, Frederick experienced rejection from significant people in his life. ("The rest of my childhood and adolescence was tough.") He also experienced homelessness. ("I was beaten and sexually abused and I spent most of the time hungry and cold.") His mother was on the streets herself, so she could not protect him. ("I hardly saw my mother, so I did not know her siblings.") ("It seemed I was alone in this world. I hated them all.")

As a child, Frederick could not understand the reasons for these hardships, which severely impacted his adult life. ("If my father was supportive, I would have been to school. It would not have taken me twenty-eight years before I got my GED.") As a result, he became defiant and refused to accept directions from people who were older than he was. In actuality, his anger was a cover for a deeper emotion of being confused about the rejection he faced throughout his life. ("I don't care about them. When I needed him he was not there.") He was angry with his father who could have guided him to be a better person.

He did not understand what was wrong with him that made him repulsive to the very people who were supposed to love and care for him. ("My father could have helped me to adjust to different experiences. There was no one to guide me. It was my entire fault.")

His confusion led to loneliness that confused him more. ("I don't even have a friend who has completed college.")

Vulnerability. Frederick's expression of anger at his family and his peers was a mask for a more aching emotion of fear. ("My friends see me as an angry man, but I don't know why I cannot control my anger.")

As a child, he had not learned to own and express his deeper emotions, so he only expressed anger, which he had learned how to do. "It is hard for me to forgive and forget." He was afraid that he was going to be abandoned again. ("I am afraid that the relationships I have will fail. If someone comes to my life and shows me love, I think they are pretending and may have some ulterior motives.")

As a result, Frederick looked for alliances and depended on individuals, hoping that with time his father would return, but all these alliances and individuals failed him and abandoned him again. ("At a point, they abandoned me, so I took to the streets again, but this time, I sold drugs.") He was vulnerable living on the streets, so he succumbed to rape and other forms of harassment. ("I was homeless, so I lived in the streets at the mercy of rapists and drug sellers.") He was angry because he believed that his life could have been better if his family had understood him and took him in. ("Family members did not play any role in my life. I struggled very hard in the cold gutters.")

Since his hurts were not exposed, they could not be healed, thus Frederick's expressions of anger continued onto adulthood. ("I would go and look for him and tell him my piece of mind. He has destroyed my life. I did not come to this world on my own—they brought me here and they think it is all a joke. They can go to hell.")

Worthlessness. Because of the abandonment experiences of his childhood, Frederick felt that everyone despised him. ("I see the world as an unfriendly place. My father and everyone else messed my life up.") As a child, the only way he knew how to deal with his experiences was to rebel because he had not then fully developed the skills to deal with his emotions properly. ("At a point, they too abandoned me, so I took to the streets again, but this time I sold drugs.") The only way he could express his feelings at that time was to defy instructions, but in actuality, Frederick was feeling worthless in the face of his abandonment. He used drugs to cover his lack of self-esteem. ("As I came out, drug peddling was all I could do.")

Frederick's feelings of worthlessness were also the result of loneliness. ("It seems I was alone in this world.") ("You carry your own burden because no one will carry it for you.") His history of early abandonment instilled in Frederick increased fear and distrust of others. ("I am sorry for my girlfriend. She loves me, and she is faithful to me, but I always accuse her of cheating on me.") His problems of connecting and closeness were due to the traumatic experiences of his childhood.

Hurt. Frederick was hurt at the way his life went in his childhood, and even though he knew there was nothing he could do about his abandonment, he became angry. ("If my father had been supportive, I would have been to school. It would not have taken me twenty-eight years before I got my GED.") He was angry with the people around him because he thought they did not understand him. ("I hated them all. My mother, my grandparents, and the Good Samaritan let me down.")

He struggled with coming to terms with his abandonment because he had not developed the skills to express his deeper emotions properly. Instead, Frederick demonstrated anger as a defense mechanism with which he covered his hurt. ("One day, my mother visited and complained to them about my weight. Instead of staying to take good care of me, she blamed them for being bad parents, so when she left my grandparents deserted me. The rest of my childhood and adolescence was tough.") He was hurt because his father could have prevented the multiple rejections he experienced in his childhood. ("My father could have helped me to adjust to different experiences.") He was hurt because he believed that with the help of individuals who came into his life, he could have learned how to get out of his situation earlier than he when he went to jail. ("I wished someone saved my life. There was no one to guide me. I could have been someone different.")

Though Frederick was hurting as a result of his pain, he struggled to let it go. He believed that by letting it go, he would have nothing to hold on to. ("It is hard for me to forgive and forget.")

CHAPTER 8
Ethan

I grew up without my father. It did not seem to be a big deal when I was a child because my mother ensured that I had everything I needed. But when I entered high school, it became a nightmare. I needed my father in my life.

My mother and father were never married, but they loved each other dearly. My father was around during my mother's pregnancy and was present during my birth. He was very excited when I was born and he carried me in his arms. My father used to take me to his parents' house about sixty miles away from my mother's family home. When I was five years old, my mother found a new boyfriend, so she asked my father not to visit us again. Thinking that her boyfriend was going to marry her, she ran away with him, leaving me with my grandmother.

My grandma was a strong woman. She never left me alone, not even for a minute. Out of frustration, my father stopped coming to see me. I lived with my grandmother, who ensured that I went to school and went to church. To her, the most important thing a child needed was education, so she found me a coach to guide me through my education.

All this time, my father did not come to see me, and I did not know where he was. I was told by his brother that he had married and moved to another state to start a family.

As for my mother, she came back when I was fifteen years old, poor and wretched due to the abuse she received at the hands of her boyfriend. She came back with my two half-brothers and was pregnant with another child. My grandmother took care of us all—my mother, myself, and my brothers.

My grandmother ensured that I completed high school and college. With my college education I was able to get a good job to care for my grandmother and my mother. My grandmother died just as I was about to get married. But her memory will forever linger on my mind. As for my mother, she married again and left our hometown. Even then, I did not see my father.

My mother had three brothers. One was a pastor, another was a teacher, and the third was a mechanic. They were good people who were married and lived with their children. They did not play any important role in my life, but whenever they were around, they instilled discipline in all the children in Grandma's house. I remember one time I had refused to do my homework and Grandma told one of my uncles; he spanked me and advised me to take my education seriously. I think I looked up to my uncles to live a life without drugs and neighborhood gangs.

My grandmother was my father, mother, and aunt. She showed me a lot of love and also taught me life lessons. At times when I thought everyone had given up on me, Grandma was there to lift me up. She used her pension money to ensure that all my needs were met. She felt that if I did not succeed in life, she would be blamed because she did not allow my father to take me along with him when he asked her to do so in the past.

My mother's two sisters did not care about other people. They were hustlers who minded their own business. My grandmother ensured that I did not get caught up in their conflicts. However, I was very close to their children, who were my cousins.

My mother went back and forth with her life. I think she needed help to move on. She was vulnerable and thought that she always needed a man to protect her, but they turned around to abuse her.

I respect women. My wife is my advisor. I trust women more than men. When a woman loves you, she will be committed to all your interests for life. She will not abandon you unless you don't respect her. I support any woman I come across, because they are vulnerable and need the support of men to do the good things that they do.

Fathers need to take care of their children for their own good. Being responsible to your children makes one responsible in life.

I did not care about the child support that was paid to my grandmother. All I needed was my father's presence and physical support. I needed him when I graduated from middle school, high school, and college. At my college graduation, I shed tears because Grandma was sick and could not attend. Though my uncles were there, and my mother was not even aware of the ceremony, the one person I wanted most to be present was my father. I wanted him to see how big I had grown and how I had made the best of the opportunities life had given me. He would have been proud of me, but would be ashamed of himself too.

I blame my father for abandoning me. He could have written to me or called me on the phone. He could have come to my school where no one would stop him, but he chose not to. He was satisfied with his new life and his family. He could have been at my wedding to support me. That time I was older and capable of making my own decisions. Maybe he felt I would have rejected him. No, I want him and I would always do.

The harm has already been done. My wife considers me as a fatherless child but a wonderful father. I blame my father for my anxiety-producing symptoms which have affected my relationship with others. I discount others when they give me compliments, because I believe they were simulated. Sometimes, I thought I didn't deserve my wife's love even though I love her dearly.

A positive self-image means that I should feel good about myself, but whether I do that or not is another question. When I look in the mirror each morning, I see a confident man, but I don't understand why I hide my confidence and fail to believe in myself. I don't want my wife to constantly see me looking in the mirror. I don't know what she would think, but it would not do me any good. I also hide my feelings from others. My wife does not know when I am sad or happy. I try to act happy for the sake of my kids. I could have been a good basketball player like my half-brother if I had not been afraid of being rejected by my coach and colleagues.

I believe I could have been more functional occupationally and socially if my father took care of me. I grew up to know that money was not everything. I need money to take care of myself, but I need people to live. My wife believes I am a good guy, but she also believes that I am full of fear. She wishes she could help, but she cannot put her finger on what my problem is. Now I cannot connect to my wife in positive ways. She loves me unconditionally, but I struggle to accept her love. I don't know what she needs to do to make me trust her. When my grandmother died, I thought there was no one else who could understand me the way I wanted to be understood.

I am critical of myself and critical of those close to me. I am capable of doing many good things, but I experience a fear of failure when I begin a new project. I don't even trust my pastor when he told me everything would be alright. It may sound ridiculous, but it's true.

He once caught me staring at him as he preached the sermon. After service, he called me to his office and confronted me with my absent-mindedness at service. When I go to work, I fear that I may be fired. I get crazy at all these situations all the time. I pretend to be okay around others at work and in church, but I hide my real feelings inside me. I am afraid these bottled-up feelings may explode one day, but I don't know how the explosion will affect my family and my friends. Did I say friends?

Friends are temporary acquaintances who can fail you any day. They are the result of living without the people who brought you to this world. This is straight out betrayal. I don't pay attention to those people. I don't think it is jealousy. But they are different from me. I see them as white people against black people. I see them as privileged and I am deprived. I am careful when I am around them, because I am defenseless. If there is trouble, they have their fathers to defend them, while I have no one to defend me. That's how people end up in jail.

Structural Interpretation of Ethan's Lived Experience

Ethan's experiences of pain and grief in his childhood were due to being abandoned by his father. The pain was compounded by the wrong choices his mother made when he was growing up. There were conflicts within Ethan's family that affected his mother's relationship with other members of her family, which in turn affected Ethan's childhood development. He was unsure of whom to interact with or avoid. Without a father to look up to, and with no positive relationship with family members, Ethan experienced a lot of pain leading to a fear of rejection or failure.

Ethan's grandmother tried to protect him from his family conflicts and the influence of his peers in the neighborhood, but this overprotection translated to a low self-esteem in his adult life. Regardless of his grandmother's protection, Ethan continued his search for his father. He wanted his father to be at his wedding and other transitions in his life. Ethan took after his grandmother's passion for caring for others, hence his career in the human services in which he directly takes care of needy individuals as he indicated during "consent" briefing.

Ethan struggled with the memory of his abandonment experiences that impacted his psychological well-being.

Though Ethan could not fully process these feelings when he was a child, he was faced with their impact when he grew up to be an adult. He hoped to be emotionally secure, be confident, and have better connections with his peers, but his past experiences of rejection by his father and by his mother's boyfriend, the overprotection from his grandmother, and the consequent peerless childhood experiences added to his pain. His anger on his failure to achieve his goals was attributed to his father's desertion, which he believed brought his present pain on him.

Ethan demonstrated feelings of low self-esteem. Sitting down with Ethan, I found him to be good looking and confident, but Ethan did not feel good about himself as he could not make proper eye contact. He struggled with keeping a realistic and positive attitude about himself and the world around him. He found it difficult to appreciate his personal traits and accomplishments, but he was able to behave responsibly toward others. He was aware that his wife loved him unconditionally, yet he found it difficult to connect with her in positive ways. He attributed all these feelings to his experience of childhood abandonment.

Composite Interpretation of Ethan's Lived Experience

Shame. Ethan was ashamed of his childhood experiences of abandonment, but he could only express his feelings as being sad. ("I grew up without my father.") ("All this time, my father did not come to see me, and I did not know where he was.") Ethan became lonely in his adolescence when he came to know the fathers of his peers. ("But when I entered high school, it became to me a nightmare. I needed my father in my life.") ("It did not seem a big deal when I was a child because my mother ensured that I had everything I needed.")

As if grieving the abandonment from his father was not enough, Ethan was also deserted by his mother. ("As for my mother, she came back when I was fifteen years old, poor and wretched due to the abuse she received at the hands of her boyfriend.")

Ethan's grief increased with the death of his grandmother who had taken charge of nurturing him after the desertion by his parents. ("When my grandmother died, I thought there was no one else who could understand me the way I wanted to be understood.") After all that his grandmother did for him, Ethan was sad that she could not be at his graduation or at his wedding. ("At my college graduation, I shed tears because Grandma was sick and could not attend.") When his grandmother died, Ethan could express only his grief, but deep inside himself, he felt shame at not being able to reciprocate the good things his grandmother did for his development. ("My grandmother was my mother, father, and aunt. She showed me a lot of love and also taught me life lessons.")

Worthlessness. When Ethan's father abandoned him and his mother went away with her new boyfriend, he felt worthless because he thought that he was unwanted, but he was able to express his feelings as being sad. ("I am critical of myself, and critical of those close to me.") ("I experience a fear of failure when I begin a new project.") ("I blame my father for abandoning me.") With pain, he recounted the distress of his childhood experiences. ("I grew up without my father.") Ethan was angry with his mother's boyfriend who convinced her to elope with him, leaving Ethan behind. ("Thinking that her boyfriend was a better man to marry, my mother ran away with him, leaving me with my grandmother.") Though his grandmother was most willing to take care of him, Ethan wanted his father to come back. ("All this time, my father did not come to see me, and I did not know where he was.")

Ethan continued to think about his father, as he viewed his peers who had their fathers in their lives as privileged. ("But they are different from me. I see them as privileged and I am deprived.") And that perception made him lose his sense of self. ("I am careful when I am around them because I am defenseless. If there is trouble, they have their fathers to defend them, while I have no one to defend me.") Being edgy and irritable, he constantly watched for faults with himself. ("When I look in the mirror each morning, I see a confident man, but I don't understand why I hide my confidence and fail to believe in myself.") ("A positive self-image means that I should feel good about myself, but whether I do that or not is another question.")

Vulnerability. Ethan feared that his relationships were temporary and that he might be abandoned again. ("I go to work and fear that I may be fired. I get crazy at all these situations all the time.") ("My wife believes I am a good guy but full of fear. Friends are temporary acquaintances who can fail you any day.")

He is afraid of failing the most important people in his life and tries very hard to please them. ("I am capable of doing many good things, but I experience a fear of failure when I begin a new project.")

Ethan has a deep religious faith but he struggles to trust God to be there for him at all times. He was even afraid that his relationship with

God was momentary. ("Hmm … I don't even trust my pastor. It may sound ridiculous, but it is true.")

He perceived everything in his life based on his earlier abandonment experiences. ("I believe I could have been more functional occupationally and socially if my father took care of me.") The betrayal he experienced from his father and mother defined how he lived life. ("They are the result of living without the person who brought you to this world. This is straight out betrayal.")

Ethan described having no sense of self because he had no one to come to his aid when there is trouble. ("I am careful when I am around them because I was defenseless. If there is trouble, they have their fathers to defend them while I have no one to defend me.")

CHAPTER 9

Arthur

I was born out of wedlock by teenage parents. At the time, my mother was sixteen years old, while my father was seventeen years old. Before my mother became pregnant, she was a cheerleader for her high school basketball team. My father was a forward on the same team. My father denied responsibility for my conception, and though a DNA test confirmed his paternity, my father refused to play any part in my upbringing.

I was an honor student in high school, and I used to hang out with friends, most of whom had their fathers in their lives. At first I used denial as a defense mechanism to cover up my angry feelings about being abandoned by my father, but with time, I felt the emptiness of being raised by a single mother.

Though my mother worked very hard to provide for me and my sisters so that we lacked nothing, I always felt a sense of being different when I was in the company of my friends. My mother was active in my basketball games and did everything to encourage me in my studies. I understood that it was not my mother's fault, but sometimes there was the temptation of blaming her for getting pregnant so early in her life. I also lived with the pain of the fact that my mother was not married to the fathers of my two younger sisters.

When I was growing up, there were no male family members in my life. My mother bought a house in the big city, so we had limited ties with our extended family. The male family members that I knew were disrespectful to females. One of my uncles never married but had multiple female partners with whom he had children who did not live with him.

As for my female family members, they were always in competition with each other. I did not have close ties with any of my three aunts because they could not offer me help when I needed it. My aunties only wanted their own children to be better in life than those of their sisters, so they cared about no one. Grandmother took care of me and my sisters when we were babies, but she hardly visited us in the big city due to her age and illness. I think that women are good people but they allow men to take undue advantage of them and later dump them. I treat my female friends and colleagues with respect and love. I believe that no child should undergo the experiences of fatherlessness that I faced.

I do not blame my father for missing out on important milestones in my life. My mother was always there for me, so I would not know the difference if my father had played a role in my life.

Sometimes, I feel I could have been a better person in life if both my father and mother were in my life. I do not know if my mother would have worked as hard as she did to take good care of me and my sisters, but I feel that my father could have made me a stronger person if he had played his fatherly role.

Living up to one's responsibilities and not indulging in crime is my conception of a positive self-image. Notwithstanding what I missed without a father, I believe that my friends respect and trust me.

Structural Analysis of Arthur's Lived Experience

Arthur encountered a lot of pain and confusion during his childhood. His pain derived from his father's denial of his mother's pregnancy. He was confused because he did not understand why his father refused to acknowledge paternity as confirmed by the DNA test.

Arthur searched for answers to the questions regarding his abandonment because he did not know if there was something wrong with him that caused his father to desert him. While Arthur recounts that he was confused with his father's motive for denying him even before he was born, he continued to search for answers from among his peers who had fathers in their lives. Psychologically, he did not accept his father's rejection, so he hung out with individuals who had their fathers in their lives in order to cover up his feelings and gain a better sense of belonging.

Additionally, Arthur was hurt by his father's decision, because he could not understand the reasons for his father's change of heart after having an intimate relationship with his mother and for the total denial of the child they conceived.

At first, Arthur expressed his pain by being defensive about his abandonment problem by keeping relationships that he hoped would give him confidence, but when he came to terms with the fact that he lived with his single mother, the reality of the rejection that he faced came back. Though his mother tried to make him forget about his pain by providing for all his needs, Arthur was not satisfied and kept searching for surrogates who could provide him fatherly love.

Another area that caused Arthur additional pain was coming to know that his sisters had different fathers who did not marry their mother. He became more confused and began to question his mother's strength.

He was hurt by the loss of his father and questioned why he did not return. He always hoped that his father would have a change of heart and come back to him. He realized that his father's absence had made him insecure. Listening to Arthur as he narrated his childhood experience of abandonment, the author realized that Arthur was less trusting in his relationships with others.

His need for a guide to teach him how to better handle strange situations and help him to be strong in the face of stressful situations increased as he grew to be an adult. Though he did not demonstrate bitterness or anger toward his father, Arthur was deeply hurt by his father's disapproval of him. He believed that if his father had been in his life, he would have been better educated and would have chosen a better career path. His uncles' negative behavior toward women was an additional source of pain for Arthur because it reminded him of the treatment his father gave to his mother.

Eventually, Arthur accepted the pain of remaining fatherless the rest of his life, but he did not want other children to go through his experiences of abandonment, so he did not give up on his search for answers. He decided to be a good father to his children and also encourage other men to do the same. He believed that through his initiative, he could find answers about the reason for his abandonment that had caused him a lot of pain and confusion.

Composite Interpretation of Arthur's Lived Experience

Loneliness. As a result of his father's denial of his conception and the subsequent denial of his paternity even though a DNA test proved it, Arthur feared that he would be abandoned again. "My father denied responsibility for my conception … My father refused to play any part in my upbringing."

Due to these childhood experiences of abandonment and alienation,

Arthur developed rejection sensitivity. "I felt the emptiness of being raised by a single mother." "I was born out of wedlock by teenage parents."

Arthur felt lonely when he was searching for answers, and he hid the fact of his abandonment, but he coped with his feelings of grief by interacting with his peers who had their fathers in their lives. "At first I used denial as a defense mechanism to cover up my angry feelings about being abandoned by my father." Though he had difficulty trusting others, he hid his real feelings by engaging in activities that he thought would help him forget his pain. "I was an honor student in high school, and I used to hang out with friends, most of whom had their fathers in their lives."

As a way of coping with his pain, Arthur avoided talking about his loss except on a very superficial level. "At first, I used denial as a defense mechanism to cover up my angry feelings of being abandoned by my father."

This behavior reinforced itself by creating situations in which Arthur perceived himself to be rejected in many ways. "I always felt a sense of being different when I was in the company of my friends." Without the answers he needed for the cause of his abandonment, Arthur felt sad as he thought about why his father denied him even before he was born. "My father refused to play any part in my upbringing."

Hurt. Arthur was hurt by his experiences of rejection by his father. "I believe that no child should undergo the experiences of fatherlessness that I faced." When he was old enough to come to terms with his childhood experiences, Arthur began to react to his feelings with anger and resentment.

He was equally hurt with the knowledge that his sisters were fatherless. "I also lived with the pain of knowing that my mother was not married to the fathers of my two sisters." He was hurt because he believed that his mother took good care of his sisters and him so that they would not feel their abandonment experiences. "I do not know if my mother would have worked as hard as she did now to take good care of me and my sisters."

Arthur was hurt by his father's denial of his mother's pregnancy, but as a child, he certainly could hardly express his real feelings about his experiences, which he expresses more clearly now as an adult. "I think that women are good people who only allow men to take undue advantage of them and dump them." "I felt the emptiness of being raised by a single mother."

Arthur was also unhappy about his life situation and felt that if he had his father in his life he would have had better opportunities in life. "Sometimes, I feel I could have been a better person in life if both my father and mother were in my life."

Vulnerability. Arthur lacked a positive male role model in his life. "When I was growing up, there were no male family members in my life." Accordingly, he was afraid of what his life was going to turn to. "I feel I could have been a better person in life if my father was in my life."

Having gone through his life with no male role models to instill discipline and promote pro-social attitudes in him, Arthur developed in himself a sense of insecurity. "I would not know the difference if my father had played a role in my life." While his mother kept an eye out for any hint of negative behaviors that he might exhibit, Arthur faced extra challenges in his childhood. "Though my mother worked very hard to provide for me and my sisters so that we lacked nothing, I always felt a sense of being different when I was in the company of my friends."

Arthur's vulnerability was increased as his uncles, who could have provided him positive examples, demonstrated irresponsible behaviors in their relationships. "Male family members were disrespectful to the females. One of my uncles never married, but he had multiple female partners with whom he had children who did not live with him."

Arthur's mother was aware that he was vulnerable in his environment, and she feared he might be influenced by the neighborhood's criminal activities, so she felt the need to shield him and his sisters from the family environment by moving them to the big city. "My mother bought a house in the big city, so we had limited ties with our extended family."

Arthur felt vulnerable in the face of having no males in his life to guide him to be a man. "I felt the emptiness of being raised by a single mother." Though he believed that his mother's protection was in the right direction, he hoped his father would return to him or his uncles would change their character and serve as positive role models for him.

CHAPTER 10
Eric

I used to be ashamed of my childhood because my mother was poor, unemployed, and sick. I did not know who my father was because my mother did not talk about him. Even when I asked about my father, my mother told me, "Don't you worry about him." As a result, I used to keep the story of my childhood a secret. I thought it made me look flawed and a failure. I thought that if my friends and colleagues knew that I did not know my father, they would stop liking me. This fear thrived on my lack of logic in this matter. I lived with this fear for more than thirty years.

My situation was worsened by the activities in the neighborhood in which I grew up. Drug abuse and armed robbery were common activities there. My mother's illness also made it worse, because sometimes I had to help her use the bathroom at the back of our living quarters. Some of my peers taunted me any time I stepped out of the house. It sounds dramatic, I know, but it is true.

I was a good student at school, so I received some material help from my teachers and my schoolmates who meant well. By the time I was a teenager, I knew what I wanted to be in the future: a pastor. This goal was driven by the need to understand the difficulties God allowed some people to go through regardless of their faith in him.

I did not know how my mother met the man who impregnated her, which led to her paralysis after I was born. All I knew was that this man left and did not return. My search for answers regarding my father did not yield results because the only person who could give me answers was my mother. But at that time, she did not talk about him, so I decided to be patient until one day when my mother would be willing to show me who my father was.

Unfortunately, my mother died when I entered Bible school. My emotions at that time were a mixture of pain and sorrow, for my mother's passing—anger for not getting answers to the question of who my father was, fear of loneliness for not knowing any family member, shame of the stigma of remaining fatherless child, and now a motherless man too.

But at my mother's memorial service, a woman introduced herself to me as my mother's only sister and said that she wanted me to meet with my biological father. Shocked and overwhelmed with grief and anxiety, I met with a good-looking man who introduced himself simply as Jacob. When I heard the words, "I am your dad," I was instantly filled with tears. I was happy at that moment, but I also felt it was too late. I felt it was late for my mother who could have confirmed if this man was really my father. It was also late for me to bond with this man who could have redirected my life goals. I felt cheated and unfairly treated by the irony of this situation. At the loss of my mother, I found what I had been looking for all my life.

It became all too clear to me that Jacob was my father because there was a clear resemblance between us, such as his soft voice and his good looks. Jacob seemed ashamed and could not make eye contact. I also realized that Jacob was remorseful, and I wished he could be bold to express it openly. After a short conversation with my aunt, Jacob returned to me, held my hands and knelt down in tears and begged for forgiveness. The pain in my father's eyes melted my heart and I forgave him.

I did not know any male family members. I had no knowledge or connection with any of my family members. In fact, the sole time I met with my mother's only sister was at my mother's funeral. My grandmother must have passed on before I was born. I did not ask about her because of my mother's illness.

Caring for my mother was the greatest challenge I faced in my life. But it built in me a genuine sense of compassion. I understood her pain. She was very fragile and had no one to support her. I was her only support. My mother's illness made me a strong person.

This also gave me the skills to love and care about others. I treat women with respect. Every female represents a part of my mother, and I do my best to help them in every possible way. I love my wife and children. I respect my colleagues just as they respect me.

I hope fathers who hear my story will take a cue from it. They need to be responsible for their children and bring them up to be successful. In this way, they can be assured of their children's help in their old age. I did not know the role of fathers until I grew up, but I think if I had received a responsible fatherhood, it would not have made a lot of difference. I forgave him the first time I met him. He apologized, and I realized he was my father no matter what, so he deserved my forgiveness. In that way, I received the blessings of the Almighty Father.

I believe that one has to be patient but steadfast in life. It is important not to judge others but to have a clear understanding of people's situation. I have gained a lot of respect for not acting harshly on others who wronged me.

Others may see me as a caring and giving person. My wife understands my pain and assists me when I am mentally occupied with it. I try my best to be supportive of others.

Without a father, I grew up to understand that I cannot take anything for granted. I am a cautious person. I think deeply before I act and I listen and accept the feedback of others in my dealings with them. I don't know how life would have been for me if I had been with my father in my childhood, but I have a strong character which I hope to impart to my children.

Structural Interpretation of Eric's Lived Experience

Eric's childhood experiences were filled with the pain of being alienated and rejected by his father. Additionally, he went through this pain with his mother who was poor and suffered from an incurable medical condition. He thought he did something wrong for his father to abandon him, because he did not know when or how his father went away. His mother's refusal to give him an insight into these questions increased his anxiety and caused him further pain.

He could only speculate as to the cause of his father's desertion. He blamed it all on himself, because he thought that his father had deserted his mother because of her paralysis that had resulted from his childbirth. Eric was physically supportive of his mother, but his primary concern was to find his father and bond with him. Since his mother was not ready to provide him the answers to his questions about his father, he chose to keep his pain within himself.

Eric was a good student, and he had a lot of friends who looked up to him for leadership, so he was worried that if his peers found out about his pain he would receive negative responses from them. This fear of rejection was a source of discomfort for him because it lowered his confidence.

Additionally, his mother's debilitating illness served as a source of embarrassment for him, because of his secreting of his real feelings about himself. He was convinced of the inevitability of rejection, so he rejected people who wanted to be part of his life.

Eric's continued search for answers regarding his paternal desertion led him to become a pastor. He wanted to find answers to the questions that no one was ready to give him, so he sought them from a spiritual source. He was sure that a better understanding of his situation would ease his worry and doubt of "not knowing."

Unfortunately, Eric's grief was increased when his mother died. Though he did not know of any of his family members, he was determined to continue with his search for answers, so he was relieved when his aunt approached him at his mother's funeral service and introduced him to his father.

With the strong religious principles imbued in him by his mother, Eric forgave his father. But Eric needed his father to be present in his life. He needed his presence—his love and affection. Eric did not need his father's apology; instead he needed his support to build the self-esteem that he had lost. He forgave his father and began the process of reconciling with him. Adhering to these principles had made him a successful pastor. His religious instincts made him believe in the will of God, so he did not question God's plan and he moved on with his life. He believed that in being patient as his mother advised, he had finally been able to get answers to the questions that had bothered him for so long.

Composite Interpretation of Eric's Lived Experience

Shame. ("I used to keep the story of my childhood a secret.") Eric had difficulty discussing his abandonment issues with his peers, because he harbored a fear that when his friends found that he grew up fatherless, they would reject him. ("I thought that if my friends and colleagues knew that I did not know my father, they would stop liking me.")

He hoped to find his father, so he kept pestering his mother for answers about who his father was. ("Even when I asked about my father, my mother would answer by saying, 'Don't you worry about him.'")

He feared that he would lose the connections he had with his peers if they knew about his pain. In this way, Eric placed his life within an inner world of shame and secrecy. ("I thought it made me look flawed and a failure.") In addition, Eric's mother's debilitating illness increased his pain. ("My mother's illness also made it worse.")

As a result, it became difficult for him to form primary relationships. He rejected those who wanted to be part of his life because he was ashamed to interact with his peers and hardly came out of the house except when he was going to school. ("Some of my peers taunted me any time I stepped out of the house.") His feelings of sadness were the masks for his inner emotions of shame and despair.

Vulnerability. As a result of his painful childhood experiences, Eric was afraid that others who knew his situation would not like him. ("If my friends and colleagues knew that I did not know my father, they would stop liking me.")

Though his mother asked him not to worry about their situation, Eric worried about their daily needs and looked up to well-meaning individuals for help. ("I was a good student at school, so I received some material help from my teachers and my schoolmates who meant well.")

His fear was driven by the anxious feeling of "not knowing" why his father left. ("I did not know how my mother met the man who impregnated her, which led to her paralysis after I was born.")

Eric felt vulnerable in social situations, so he did not participate in them. ("I thought that if my friends and colleagues knew that I did not know my father, they would stop liking me. This fear thrived on my lack of logic in this matter. I lived with this fear for more than thirty years.")

Eric hoped that one day his father was going to show up, but he lived with this uncertainty through his childhood and adolescence. ("All I knew was that this man left and never came back.")

Eric also feared that he might be influenced by the negative behavior of his peers in his neighborhood, and this made him feel vulnerable. ("My situation was worsened by the activities in the neighborhood in which I grew up. Drug abuse and armed robbery were common activities.")

His fears stemmed from the realization that he did not fit in well with the other children he knew. The low self-esteem that accrued from it made him feel unwanted.

Confusion: Eric searched for strategies to address the loss of his father from abandonment and the loss of his mother to severe illness. He hoped to gain a better insight into his painful early childhood experiences, but he was unsuccessful. He became increasingly confused with what he wanted to do with himself, so with a pervasive belief and trust in God, he sought divine intervention. ("By the time I became a teenager, I had known what I wanted to be in the future: a pastor." "This goal was driven by the need to understand the difficulties God allowed some people to go through regardless of their faith in Him.")

From the time when he was young, Eric bottled up his feelings because he knew that by expressing them, he would compound his pain. Even when he tried without success to get answers from his mother, Eric kept his pain to himself and prayed and hoped that one day, his mother was going to let him know who his father was. ("My search for my father did not yield answers because the only person who could give me answers was my mother. So I decided to be patient until one day when my mother would be willing to show me who my father was.")

Loneliness. Eric's mother's death increased that pain that he had been harboring for so long. He became lonely because he had lost the only person who was close to him and cared about him. He was lonely because he did not know any of his mother's relatives. He was lonely because he did not know any of his mother's relatives. His loneliness was also as a result of not having peers who knew what he had gone through in his young life, but most importantly, because he had lost his mother who was the only person who could have answered his questions about his paternity. ("Unfortunately, my mother died when I entered Bible school.")

He was afraid of the future, but he hid his emotion by grieving his mother's death. ("My emotions at that time were a mixture of pain and sorrow, for my mother's passing—anger for not getting answers to the question of who my father was, fear of loneliness for not knowing any family member, shame of the stigma of remaining fatherless child, and now a motherless man too.") Underneath the sad facade was an emotion of fear that Eric had not learned to own and express.

CHAPTER 11
Charles

My name is Charles. I am the third of three children. My parents strove very hard to provide my older siblings with the opportunities they needed to grow and become successful adults, but my parents died before I went to high school. At that time, my brother and sister had already grown into adulthood, so they returned to their families, abandoning me with no other close relative to care for me. My brother was a policeman and my sister was a nurse. I wondered why they could not support me at least through high school.

I grieved a lot, and I could not attend school. One of my teachers noted my repeated absences from school, and when I had time to go to class, he noticed that I had difficulty attaching to the other students. I withdrew from my friends and extracurricular activities. I developed depression and anxiety. In fact, I felt that I had lost everything that was most important, time and time again.

As a result of these multiple, repetitive losses, people and things began to lack meaning to me. I became suicidal and started cutting myself. I also engaged in risk-taking behaviors including using illicit drugs and gambling. One of my high school teachers took me to live with him, but I left when he started to sexually molest me.

At this time, I felt there was no need to live. I began to live in the streets, selling drugs. I sold drugs not because I needed money but because I needed a companion. I needed someone who could relate to my situation. Unfortunately, my mentor who was providing me with drugs to peddle was arrested and jailed for one year.

I took advantage of his absence to rent a room, and I had a girlfriend. I used the proceeds from the drug peddling to keep myself busy going to nightclubs and betting on basketball matches. When my mentor returned from jail I could not render a successful account of my stewardship, so he became angry. He seized the property that I had acquired, and he chased me out of my apartment.

Living on the streets at that time was difficult after I had tasted a life of comfort. I was scared for my life. I could neither find a room to live in nor be on the streets because my mentor was constantly on my heels requesting his money. I met an old lady on the streets who took me to her home. She lived alone, and she found me a janitor job at the aged persons' home where her sister lived. Due to my past experiences of close relatives abandoning me or taking advantage of me, I was uncomfortable living in my newly found home.

My new friend introduced me to her church. I found in the church a place of refuge. Each Sunday, I attended Mass and stayed there until all three masses had ended. After each mass I stayed in the rectory where I thought I was safe until the next mass began and stayed on until the next mass and until every person left the premises. Once the parish priest asked me why I always stayed around for three masses, but I answered that I had nothing else to do and nowhere else to go to.

I joined the local gym and each day I went there; I paid extra to be allowed to stay there until I could leave for work. Sometimes I went to work even when I was not scheduled to do so and worked on those days voluntarily.

I did all these things to run from my fears. I was afraid I was going to lose my job, even though my supervisor had a positive regard for me. I left my girlfriend because I feared she was going to expose me to my mentor. My experiences have jeopardized the opportunity for me to develop secure attachments and trusting relationships with adults. I refused to disclose my identity to the lady in whose house I lived because I did not trust her. I did not talk about my parents' death, nor did I talk about my brother and sister. Now I live like someone running from the police, even though I have done nothing wrong.

I don't know why I am telling my story, but in a way it has given me some relief. At least someone has listened to me without judging me. In fact, I now understand the importance of relating and attaching emotionally to others, but I still feel that the harm has already been done and has affected my whole being.

Structural Interpretation of Charles's Lived Experience

Charles had been running from a world that he thought was unfriendly to him. From his childhood, Charles perceived his close relatives as unfriendly for not accepting him. He was abandoned after the death of his parents. As a young person, Charles thought that his siblings could take care of him. But they deserted him. Charles missed his family, which was intact until the death of both parents. He sought authority figures who could guide him in the absence of close relatives.

The only place he could find companionship was in the streets. But life in the streets came with its price of risky behaviors and crime. His problems were compounded by the incarceration of his drug-selling mentor. Charles thought he was able to live on his own, but he sank deeper into trouble. Charles's problems increased when his mentor returned from jail and was dissatisfied with the results of Charles's drug peddling.

Charles could not stay at any one place. He hid in churches, gymnasiums, and at work. He did not trust anyone for fear of being handed over to his menacing mentor. He was scared day to day but could not confide in anybody.

His pain of running from his mentor reminded him of the need for his parents and siblings. But none of them was present. Charles could not even confide in the parish priest, nor could he trust the lady with whom he was staying. Because he thought that his girlfriend could betray him, Charles severed his relationship with her.

Composite Interpretation of Charles's Lived Experience

Confusion: After the deaths of his parents and the desertion by his siblings, Charles suffered from a feeling of not being good enough, and he struggled to come to terms with why they abandoned him. Charles developed depression and anxiety because of his sense of abandonment and confusion. ("As a result of these multiple, repetitive losses, people and things began to lack meaning to me. I became suicidal and started cutting myself. I also engaged in risk-taking behaviors including using illicit drugs and gambling.")

Charles was confused with his situation because before his parents died, the family was intact. He could relate with his brother and sister in positive ways, so he wondered if he had done something wrong for them to desert him at such a critical stage in his development. ("I am the third of three children. My parents strove very hard to provide my older siblings with the opportunities they needed to grow and become successful adults, but they died before I went to high school.")

Loneliness: Throughout his adolescence, Charles felt lonely. He hoped that someone could come to his aid in those difficult times of emotional distress, but his siblings abandoned him.

In his loneliness, Charles felt that he had lost all that mattered in his life. ("In fact, I felt that I had lost everything that was most important, time and time again.") He had been rejected by his own siblings, so he believed that no one else would accept him. The life he wanted to live was not within his immediate power because of the loss of his primary attachments. ("As a result of these multiple, repetitive losses, people and things began to lack meaning to me. I became suicidal and started cutting myself.")

Charles felt isolated so was afraid to meet the world. ("Each Sunday, I attended Mass and stayed there until all three masses had ended. After each mass I stayed in the rectory where I thought I was safe until the next mass began and stayed on until the next mass and until every person left the premises.")

Shame: As an abandoned child, Charles had difficulty forming primary relationships. This was the result of the underlying abandonment pain. In his bid to gain self-acceptance, Charles severed those relationships that he had already formed. ("My experiences have jeopardized the opportunity for me to develop secure attachments and trusting relationships with adults.") He severed his various relationships so that he could be left alone to live with his wound. ("I did all these things to run from my fears.")

He also had no trust for secure attachments because the most important people in his life severed their attachments with him without good reasons. As a result, he became afraid of the people who wanted to help him. ("I was afraid I was going to lose my job, even though my supervisor had a positive regard for me.") Charles engaged in activities that hid him from the limelight. ("Sometimes I went to work even when I was not scheduled to do so and worked on those days voluntarily. I did all these things to run from my fears.")

Additionally, he felt that he could be betrayed by close friends just as he had been abandoned by his siblings and other family members. ("I left my girlfriend because I feared she was going to expose me to my mentor.") He also felt he was less attractive to those around him, and this made him run from his friends. ("Now I live like someone running from the police, even though I have done nothing wrong.")

Charles came to realize that he was going to live with shame wounding throughout his life. He did not, however, understand how this inner world of shame operated, and this unconscious mental pain produced a lot of negative energy for him. ("I don't know why I am telling my story, but in a way it has given me some relief. At least someone has listened to me without judging me.")

Hurt: Charles was hurt because of the way his siblings treated him after their parents died. ("I wondered why they could not support me at least through high school.") He felt betrayed by his family members because he expected that someone from his family could have cared for him until he completed high school, but no one did. ("I wondered why they could not support me through high school.") He expressed his pain by refusing to go to school. ("I grieved a lot, and I could not attend school.")

Vulnerability: Charles believed that he was susceptible to future negative responses and unprotected from danger and misfortune. ("Due to my past experiences of close relatives abandoning me or taking advantage of me, I was uncomfortable living in my newly found home.") Furthermore, Charles felt anxious and had feelings of fear and apprehension. His limited financial resources made him feel threatened by his environment. ("Sometimes I went to work even when I was not scheduled to do so and worked on those days voluntarily.")

The absence of relatives and close family friends who could help him through his emotional stages after his parents' deaths made Charles feel vulnerable. ("I needed someone who could relate to my situation.")

What activated Charles's sense of vulnerability was not the fact that he was in danger but rather his feeling that someone out there was out to get him. ("Now I live like someone running from the police, even though I have done nothing wrong.")

Worthlessness: Charles experienced feelings of worthlessness, so it became more difficult for him to imagine feelings of relevance and consequence. ("Once the parish priest asked me why I stayed around for three masses, but I answered that I had nothing else to do and nowhere else to go to.")

Charles withdrew from relationships and began using drugs and alcohol. He became lethargic, with diminished emotional expressions. ("I became suicidal and started cutting myself. I also engaged in risk-taking behaviors including using illicit drugs and gambling.")

Even though Charles faced significant problems in regard to his friends and his environment, he was preoccupied with worry about insignificant problems, problems that made him feel worthless and unaccepted. ("I was afraid I was going to lose my job, even though my supervisor had a positive regard for me.")

CHAPTER 12
Group Interpretations of the Narratives

The analysis and interpretations of the stories of Garcon, Leon, Lawrence, Perry, Dontae, Peter, Frederick, Ethan, Arthur, Eric, and Charles divulged their experiences of deeper emotions that they had not learned to own and express. These stories revealed a recurrence of the following primary emotions that the individuals masked with secondary feelings to justify their experiences: (a) confusion, (b) loneliness, (c) shame, (d) hurt, (e) vulnerability, and (f) worthlessness. (It was evident that these men were searching for compensating methods to address their losses).

Confusion

Most of the men experienced a plethora of emotional troubles in their childhood that affected their development into adolescence and adulthood. In most cases they were suddenly abandoned, so they experienced shock and confusion. These experiences made them feel that their fathers' actions were a result of something they did wrong, and this led them to feel guilt and even fear.

They were overwhelmed with several emotions but were able to express only the underlying physiological and cognitive factors of their inner subjective experiences. In these situations, their expressions of anger and fear were masks for the inner core emotions that they were too confused to own and express. Their fear was driven by their early childhood wounds and emotional trauma from their early childhood that made them feel confused. As children, these men had been incapable of seeing themselves as separate from their fathers and believing that they had worth as individuals apart from their fathers. The only reality that they knew was the reality they grew up in—that of being deserted by their fathers. The men demonstrated that they had fewer psychological tools that could help them to heal.

The lack of healthy role models prevented them from learning to overcome their fear. Their early childhood wounds caused them to feel that there was something wrong with their beings, and that pain caused them to be confused.

> **Garcon:** *"The alienation my mother and I faced from my father's family is inexplicable. It seemed like he vanished into thin air. He was very close to me, so when he left without telling me anything, I was devastated."*

> **Leon:** *"My mother's friends were prostitutes; they came to our room, smoked marijuana, and formulated their solicitation plans for the next night."*

> **Lawrence:** *"I have known about my father all my life, but I met him for the first time when I was twenty-eight years old."*

> **Perry:** *"But who can give this kind of love except God Almighty. I find it difficult to deal with ideas and fears of failing in my duties*

as a protector, leader, and the strong yet sensitive one." "A father should take charge of making childrearing decisions and even assume custody of their children in case of a marital separation; in short, a father should be the strong force in his family and in his community, bringing up his own children in positive ways and helping to bring up others in the community."

Dontae: *"I have fought with myself for so long for feeling like no one could love me because of the rejection I've felt due to my dad leaving. The damage of my childhood experiences has formed my personality and affected the way I feel inside."*

Peter: *"I don't know if I should say I had a good childhood."*

Frederick: *"My friends see me as an angry man, but I do not understand why I cannot control my anger."*

Eric: *"My search for my father did not yield answers because the only person who could give me answers was my mother. So I decided to be patient until one day when my mother would be willing to show me who my father was."*

Charles: *"As a result of these multiple, repetitive losses, people and things began to lack meaning to me. I became suicidal and started cutting myself. I also engaged in risk-taking behaviors including using illicit drugs and gambling."*

Loneliness

For participants in the study, loneliness was a result of their need for warm, physically affectionate, and tender relationships with their fathers, a need that was not fulfilled earlier in their childhood. When they were abandoned early in their lives, the participants did not have levels of maturity that allowed them to live independently of their fathers, so they experienced difficulties in resolving their emotional traumas. The lack of joyful, gentle fatherly love from the time they were little boys made them feel unwanted and empty. In their minds, they felt lonely even when other persons loved them. They had not learned to accept and own their inner feeling of emptiness that was caused by the gradual accumulation of the unfinished mental and emotional business of self-actualization.

The absence of fathers who could be physically affectionate to them or communicate their love to them also caused fear of rejection in the participants. Unrecognized and untreated emotional wounds of loneliness from their early lives produced feelings of disconnectedness in participants' adult lives that affected their intimate relationships.

Participants' descriptions of experiences of desertion showed that they could not openly express their feelings of anger, so they attempted to control their emotional pain by denying that they felt alone. They thought that their sadness was the result of their adult life experiences or commitments, so they relived the old experiences, judging every current experience in the light of the old one and closing avenues for new experiences.

Participants either ignored or denied their earlier years of loneliness that arose from the severe emotional disappointments during their childhood and adolescence because they were not able to recognize the actual origins of their emotional difficulties.

> **Garcon:** *"I have been searching for my father from as early as when I was four years old. I kept searching for him in other father*

figures." "The sense of loss that I experienced led me to have faith in God."

Leon: *I don't think I had a family. I knew two of my mother's sisters, but they were different from my mother. One of them was a teacher, and the other was married and lived with her husband back in our hometown. But they hardly spoke to us." "There have not been female family members in my life."*

Lawrence: *"She hardly paid attention to me when he was present, so I did not like him. In a way, he was the cause of my mother's hatred for my father."*

Dontae: *"A child without a father is like a lost sheep … I felt lost many times." "The damage of my childhood experiences has formed my personality and affected the way I feel inside." "When I asked my mother for things and she could not afford them, there was no other person to fall on."*

Peter: *"My mother was not much in my life; she was busy with her own life." "I think there was a need for positive male role models in the family." "Most of my uncles who lived in our house drank and smoked."*

Arthur: *"I felt the emptiness of being raised by a single mother." "I was born out of wedlock by teenage parents."*

Eric: *"Unfortunately, my mother died when I had entered Bible school." "My emotions at that time were a mixture of pain and sorrow, for my mother's passing—anger for not getting answers to the question of who my father was, fear of loneliness for not knowing any family member, shame of the stigma of remaining* *fatherless child, and now a motherless man too.*

Charles: *"In fact, I felt that I had lost everything that was most important, time and time again."*

Shame

Most participants described painful emotions of unhealthy guilt. As children, they did not understand that their guilt feelings emanated from an internalized shame that was directly connected with the fear of their abandonment. Participants perceived themselves as having done something wrong in their childhood that made their fathers abandon them. They carried this sense of guilt from their childhood to their adulthood because they had not learned to shed their fear of abandonment. The shame that they felt was accompanied by a sense of inadequacy that was caused by the disruption of the interpersonal bond that should have existed between them and their fathers. Participants' feelings were traceable to their sense of need for protection from their fathers and to be accepted by others.

Since they were deprived of this connectedness early in their childhood, participants developed an internal state of grief that was accompanied by feelings of shame. These internalized emotions impaired participants' ability to develop and sustain positive self-worth and to form meaningful adult relationships.

Their emotions were directly caused by their fathers' absence. Their reactions led them to reject the importance of forming relationships, and that resulted in fettering themselves to the position of denial and unresolved grief.

Garcon: *"As a child, I hid the fact of my father's desertion; it* *seemed to me that I was the cause of that action."*

Leon: *"My family was stigmatized by the many incarcerations of my cousins and uncles." "As long as I could remember, the males from my family were all in prison." "As I was entering prison, my mother was getting out of jail."*

Perry: *"It is ridiculous that I am not able to exhibit a sense of benevolent responsibility to lead as a pastor and a father." "I am not able to provide for and protect my family and my flock in ways appropriate to a man's differing relationships."*

Dontae: *"They gave me a kick in the gut, lowered my self-esteem and made me feel worthless. I am different in many ways. At my age I feel I am too shy to attend social functions."*

Ethan: *"I try struggling to accept compliments from others. I think they are just mocking me." "I don't want my wife to constantly see me looking in the mirror." "I see them as privileged and I am deprived."*

Eric: *"I used to be ashamed of my childhood because my mother was poor, unemployed, and sick." "I thought that if my friends and colleagues knew that I did not know my father, they would stop liking me." "I thought it made me look flawed and a failure."*

Charles: *"My experiences have jeopardized the opportunity for me to develop secure attachments and trusting relationships with adults."*

Hurt

Some participants demonstrated anger at their fathers for having abandoned them in their childhood. Their expressions were ways for drawing attention away from their feelings of hurt. Participants covered their hurt of being abandoned by their fathers, because they had not matured enough to react to their emotional responses to their pain.

They did not acknowledge their unfulfilled needs and longing for their fathers, so they remained in turmoil about themselves and their intimate relationships. The lack of positive role models also hurt participants. They were frustrated when they did not have positive male role models to teach them life lessons in the absence of their fathers.

Most of their male family members were also absent or they engaged in nonconforming behaviors. Refusing to acknowledge their unfulfilled needs and longings for their fathers, participants' pain stayed in their subconscious as they matured into adulthood. They remembered their hurt with fear as they attempted to fill the gaps regarding their abandonment. Their experiences of fear of abandonment were disempowering and uncomfortable, so anger was the most fundamental reaction to their hurt, which, being unhealed, could not be exposed.

> **Garcon:** *"He was very close to me, so when he left without telling me anything, I was devastated."*

> **Leon:** *"I had traumatic childhood experiences. I don't think I had a family. I suffered a lot to get here." "That was the devil that destroyed all our lives."*

> **Lawrence:** *"My father left when I was a child so I did not experience his protection and care." "She hardly paid attention to me when he was present, so I did not like him." "I missed him when*

my mother's boyfriend refused to answer some of my questions."

Perry: *"Honestly, there was no one to look up to or to show me how things were supposed to be done." "What they do not know is my inner struggles to be a man. Until I am able to feel that I could be loved and accepted by others, my feelings will remain the same."*

Frederick: *"My father and everyone else messed my life up." "I don't remember what happened, but they abandoned me at that age. The rest of my childhood and adolescence was tough."*

Arthur: *"I believe that no child should undergo the experiences of fatherlessness that I faced." "Sometimes, I feel I could have been a better person in life if both my father and mother were in my life."*

Charles: *"I wondered why they could not support me at least through high school. I grieved a lot, and I could not attend school."*

Vulnerability

All participants in the study felt unprotected in their childhood, so they feared talking about their true feelings. They carried these feelings throughout their childhood and adolescence and even into their adult lives. Despite logical assurances from their partners that all would be well, these men dreaded being rejected again in their adult relationships. These childhood experiences made participants feel unworthy of the love of their partners or others who wanted to be part of their lives.

They were convinced that they were inevitably going to be rejected, so they rebuffed others before they got abandoned again.

Participants knew that they were vulnerable to sudden unwanted changes, so they always felt shaky and demonstrated extreme fear. All of the men had difficulty developing and sustaining self-esteem, recognizing their feelings, and being expressive with their wives and children, because the desertion by their fathers had been sudden and inexplicable. They did not understand why their fathers abandoned them without offering explanations. The men hid their feelings and motives from others, because not even their mothers had been able to explain their fathers' motivation for deserting them.

> **Garcon:** *"I succumbed to pressure from peers to use substances in my adolescence." "I kept looking for him in other father figures." "The only male figures that were close to me impacted my life in negative ways."*

> **Leon:** *"I liken my childhood experiences to a child crawling toward a fireplace. He needs a mother or a father to stop him from getting hurt, but I had no one like that, so I got hurt."*

> **Lawrence:** *"When it became clear to me that my mother did not want me to contact my father, I was wounded and felt unsafe."*

> **Perry:** *"I never had a member of my family playing the role of a role model in my life." "But he was never there, and the thought of that has affected my psychological frame."*

> **Dontae:** *"Each day, I experienced the care of a different woman." "Some of these experiences were good, but most of the time, I felt lonely and abused." "A child without a father is like a lost sheep."*

Peter: *"She told me, 'You and your sisters are not safe in this neighborhood.' So she wanted to send me out of there before I joined those 'junkies.'"*

Frederick: *"I was homeless, so I lived in the streets at the mercy of rapists and drug sellers." "I was beaten and sexually abused and I spent most of the time hungry and cold."*

Ethan: *"I am careful when I am around them, because I am defenseless. If there is trouble, they have their fathers to defend them, while I have no one to defend me."*

Arthur: *"I felt the emptiness of being raised by a single mother." "When I was growing up, there were no male family members in my life."*

Eric: *"My situation was worsened by the activities in the neighborhood in which I grew up. Drug abuse and armed robbery were common activities. My mother's illness also made it worse, because sometimes I had to help her use the bathroom at the back of our living quarters."*

Charles: *"Due to my past experiences of close relatives abandoning me or taking advantage of me, I was uncomfortable living in my newly found home."*

Worthlessness

The stories of these eleven men showed that being worthless meant having a low level of confidence in their intelligence and abilities. As a result of being abandoned by their fathers early in their childhood,

John Attram, PhD

the men had difficulties making decisions and undertaking complex projects on their own. Most of them demonstrated pessimism and self-doubt and belittled their own accomplishments. They shied away from responsibility in church and home settings. These men were uneasy being alone and were preoccupied with the fear of being abandoned or rejected by their close friends or partners. They relived the humiliation of their childhood abandonment, so they carried significant doubts about their abilities to perform tasks independently of their wives or close friends. The men were also suspicious of others who came to their aid to offer them help, because in their minds, no one could be trusted.

They portrayed helplessness that elicited caregiving behavior from their wives. Though participants were able to marry, at the core of their relationships was the feeling that they were somehow defective, unlovable, and unworthy because of their childhood emotional traumas.

They internalized these feelings from their childhood and used them to serve as defense systems to protect them from being betrayed and abandoned again. But as long as they kept reacting unconsciously to their childhood emotional wounds, participants continued to repeat these patterns. The longing for their absent fathers was intense, so they depended on sources of authority such as alliances with their churches, grandmothers, and mothers, hoping that their fathers would return.

> **Leon:** *"When I was in prison, I learned one thing, that is, those men were reduced to low-class human beings. Most of them were very smart guys, but their independence had been seized."*

> **Dontae:** *"Even with my training of speaking in public places, I find it difficult to make eye contact." "I grew most of the time not knowing who I was. I was not sure what was going to happen to me next."*

124

Peter: *"I look different from my peers, because I feel unimportant and worthless on certain occasions."*

Frederick: *"My father and everyone else messed my life up." "All my buddies are in the streets. I don't even have a friend who has completed college."*

Ethan: *"I believe I could have been more functional occupationally and socially if my father took care of me." "I experience a fear of failure when I begin a new project."*

Charles: *"Once the parish priest asked me why I stayed around for three masses, but I answered that I had nothing else to do and nowhere else to go to."*

TOO SCARED OF
TOMORROW

Some clients are unable to articulate their lived experiences as they pursue therapy for low self-esteem or anxiety. Even those clients who can articulate their experiences might manifest their inner emotions in some variety of ways. Thus, regardless of a clinician's chosen frame of reference for understanding clients' experiences, it is important to be attuned to the possibility that clients and family members have inner emotions they are not aware of, do not accept, or do not express.

Resolution of these inner emotions may strengthen clients' abilities to face and endure the changes that the anxiety or angry feelings impose upon them. Counselors are in a primary position to reflect back the need for fathers to their clients and help them transcend their defenses against the importance of their relationships.

The relationship between the recurrent group themes shown in the composite interpretation of each of the men's narratives in chapters 1 through 11 and the structural interpretation of their descriptions as a group in chapter 12 revealed a constant representation of their lived experiences. As these men narrated their experiences of growing up in fatherless families, an understanding of their emotions was gained that these men harbored an underlying fear that they had not learned to own and express.

Noted psychologist and personality theorist Silvan Tomkins

considered fear as a primary emotion that does not need specific cognitive skills for its emergence (Tomkins 1963). In other words, self-referential behavior is not necessary for the emergence of fear but is necessary for the emergence of secondary emotions such as shame, hurt, confusion, vulnerability, and worthlessness. Fathers are needed in children's lives, and a paternal absence can produce long-term effects of such secondary emotions that pose difficulties in achievement and goal-oriented behavior.

Developmental psychology experts inform us that the attachment relationships of children and their parents play a central role in children's social and emotional development (Seiffert, Hoffnung, and Hoffnung 2000). From the early developmental stages through adolescence, children require parents who support their efforts to navigate their world and who appreciate their limitations and need for restraints that ensure their physical and emotional safety and protect their self-esteem (Orbuch, Thornton, and Cancio 2000). Since parental support is not predictable and guaranteed in many cases, persons develop a fear and avoid future interactions where they believe the possibility of rejection exists (Teyber 1997).

J. D. Laird said that pain is activated in human beings when they intuitively recognize that they have a physical or emotional vulnerability. Their instinctive response to such pain includes how they treat each other (Laird 1974). Laird also said that upon realizing that they can be hurt by the disapproval of others, their fear instincts encourage them to hide that vulnerability from the view of others out of concern of being exploited.

The most important finding of my interactions with these men is that they demonstrated intense emotions regarding their losses. As a result, they perceived themselves as being vulnerable throughout their lives. Perloff (1983, 44) defined *perceived vulnerability* as "a belief that one is susceptible to future negative outcomes and unprotected from danger and misfortune." She went on to explain that "accompanying this cognition is an affective component, consisting of feelings of anxiety, fear, and apprehension." These characteristics were evident in the men's recollections of their experiences of abandonment that strongly influenced their life paths. From the time they realized that they had been abandoned, the men in this study felt betrayed by their fathers and subsequently developed painful feelings toward themselves and suspicion about later relationships.

Wade (1995) suggested that children of absent fathers can experience feelings of abandonment that can shape their lives. Likewise, the men profiled in this book knew they had no fathers while they were still young, and as they could hardly make sense of their situations, they felt the impact. The physical and emotional needs of these men can better be understood by considering the importance of emotional attachment and feelings of acceptance. Clarke-Stewart and Brentano (2006) suggested that children experienced pain in the early developmental stages because of the lack of emotional and physical attachment to their fathers.

Clarke-Stewart and Brentano concluded in their study that children's feelings were connected to their need for their fathers' protection and the need to be accepted by others. Since the men profiled in this book were deprived of this connectedness early in their childhoods, they developed painful emotions that were captured in their descriptions. These internalized emotions impaired the participants' abilities to develop and sustain positive self-worth and to form meaningful adult relationships. Almost all of the men turned to other sources of support and authority to replace the loss of their biological fathers, hoping that such shifts would help them cope with their hurt. When they were children, the men did not understand that their feelings emanated from internalized states that were directly connected with their fear of abandonment.

Damasio (1995) postulated that emotions are a powerful indicator of the personal resonance of culturally and physiologically influenced circumstances. The emotions of the men in this study were based on how they perceived themselves as having done something wrong in their childhoods that made their fathers abandon them. Consequently, they carried this sense of guilt into their adulthoods since they had not learned to shed this viewpoint. Their perceptions led to feelings of inadequacy as a result of the disruption of the interpersonal bond that should have existed between their fathers and them.

From a phenomenological perspective, emotions and cognitions are closely interrelated as aspects of how human beings participate in the world (Hertz 2002). What emerged from the analysis of the experiences of the eleven men in this study were the powerful ways in which fatherlessness undermined their senses of self. Perceived sources of emotional pain can lead to a person's loss of self. This pain can come from a variety of sources. Bachman (2000) indicated that abandoned children faced additional pain when they were growing up because they were aware that no one would be there for them and understand them.

In the same vein, Hetherington, Bridges, and Insabella (1998) found that abandoned adolescents experience greater difficulty in establishing intimate relationships than those who had their fathers in their lives. The majority of the men in this book indicated that the major impact of fatherlessness on them was their own lack of trust for significant others in their lives, which made it difficult for them to hold close and intimate relationships in their adulthoods. They described their relationships as being less than close, indicating that they had a hard time believing that anyone could love them. Additionally, Rohner and Veneziano (2001) stated that a father's involvement in a child's life potentially contributes to the child's healthy development.

In their stories, some men in this book admitted to having developed obnoxious personalities, looking confident and in control, but they recognized that this was a way of keeping others at bay—rejecting the others before they were themselves rejected. Consequently, they directed their fears inward, and that resulted in self-defeating behaviors such as withdrawing socially, abusing substances, and developing low self-esteem. For example, the men demonstrated anger as a reaction to feelings of fear of abandonment or worthlessness.

Children develop a fear of abandonment when their needs are not consistently met, which makes them develop anxiety or attempt to become emotionally self-sufficient (Bowlby 1980). These men felt humiliated by their parents in their developmental years, so they carried significant doubts about their traits and abilities to perform tasks and take on new responsibilities. Reflecting on their childhood pain of abandonment, the men realized that they had grown to be incompetent to react to complex stimuli and be more trusting in their relationships with others. The patterns of attachment developed in infancy shape aspects of personality and are reflected in subsequent significant relationships throughout individuals' lives (Danielle 1985). Interactions with these men revealed that the need for their fathers was strongly felt when they failed in their searches for male authority figures to guide and teach them how to better handle strange situations and help them to be strong in the face of stressful situations. This need increased as they grew to be to be adults.

Health care professionals should extend Bowlby's (1980) postulation that the search for the *mother* is innate so as to also consider that the search for the *father* may be an innate attribute of the child. From the stories of these men, it was clear that the need for the father is at the center of the personality that orients the child to an understanding of its need to belong and to engage in meaningful and empathetic relationships.

Kaufman and Ziegler (1987) explored the causes of violence in intimate relationships and explained that they were largely due to the experience and observation of the phenomenon in the family of origin during childhood. As described by Bandura (1977), human beings are not born with predetermined patterns of behavior. Instead, behaviorists believe that behavior is learned and that new patterns of behavior are learned by direct experience or by witnessing the behavior of others. Sellers, Cochran, and Branch (2005) studied partner violence and concluded that through a direct modeling effect, similarities across generations regarding antisocial behaviors of male children are in part a function of socioeconomic characteristics being transmitted across generations. Similarly, Akers (2009) posited that individuals emulate the behavior of people they respect, admire, and frequently observe as role models, such as their parents and religious leaders. In Akers's view, this observational learning process is important during childhood and is responsible for intergenerational transmission of behaviors. Congruent with this assertion, Maestripieri (2005) found that children who observed abusive behavior between their parents and between their parents and other family members were more likely to imitate and get accustomed to those behaviors.

In Maestripieri's study, he used female rhesus macaques in an experimental cross-fostering study, and found similar results in intergenerational transmission of behavior in a study of maternal abuse of offspring. This indicates that child maltreatment is not unique to humans but has been observed in some nonhuman primates as well. Results of this study also suggested that the intergenerational transmission of infant abuse is the result of early experience and not genetic inheritance. Maestripieri's study suggested that early adverse experience may predispose individuals to display later abusive parenting. Whether abused individuals are particularly vulnerable or resilient, however, may depend on the presence of protective factors that may be biological, or on other risk factors, or on both.

The narratives of the eleven men who grew up in fatherless families showed that individuals who go through such experiences demonstrate intense emotions regarding their losses. Such persons consider themselves susceptible to future negative outcomes and feel unprotected from danger and misfortune. This cognition is accompanied by feelings of anxiety, fear, and apprehension which are difficult to express. This finding will help counselors in planning intervention strategies for fatherless children adolescents and children who present with poor anger management and low self esteem problems.

REFERENCES

Bodenhorn, H. 2007. "Single Parenthood and Childhood Outcomes in Mid-Nineteenth-Century Urban South." *Journal of Interdisciplinary History* 38 (1), 33–64.

Bowlby, J. 1980. Attachment and Loss. Vol. 3 of *Loss: Sadness and Depression*. New York: Basic Books.

Clarke-Stewart, A., and Brentano, C. 2006. *Divorce: Causes and Consequences*. New Haven, CT: Yale University Press.

Creswell, J. W. 2007. *Qualitative Inquiry and Research Design: Choosing among Five Approaches*, 2nd ed. Thousand Oaks, CA: Sage.

Damasio, A. 1995. *Descartes' Error: Emotion, Reason, and the Human Brain*. New York: Avon Hearst.

Hertz, R. 2002. "The Father as an Idea: A Challenge to Kinship Boundaries by Single Mothers." *Symbolic Interaction* 25: 1–31.

Hetherington, E. M., Bridges, M., and Insabella, G. M. 1998. "What Matters? What Does Not? Five Perspectives on the Association between Marital Transitions and Children's Adjustment." *American Psychologist* 53: 167–184.

Hubner, S. R., and Ratzan, D. M., eds. 2009. *Growing Up Fatherless in Antiquity*. Cambridge, England: Cambridge University Press.

Kamark, E. C., and Galston, W. A. 1990. *Putting Children First: A Progressive Family Policy for the 1990s*. Washington, DC. Progressive Policy Institute, 14–15. As cited in D. Blankenhorn, *Fatherless America: Confronting Our Most Urgent Social Problem*, 31. New York: Basic Books.

Kreider, R. M., and Fields, J. 2005. *U.S. Census Bureau Current Population Reports: Living Arrangements of Children*. http:// www.census.gov/prod/2005pubs/p70–104.pdf.

Laird, J. D. (1974). "Self-Attribution of Emotion: The Effects of Expressive Behavior on the Quality of Emotional Experience." *Journal of Personality and Social Psychology* 29 (4): 475–486.

Mastripieri, D. (2005). "Early experience affects the intergenerational transmission of infant abuse in rhesus monkeys." *National Academy of Sciences 102 (27):9726-9729.*

National Fatherhood Initiative. 1996. *Father Facts*. Lancaster, PA.

O'Neill, J., and Hill, M. A. 2003. *Gaining Ground, Moving Up: The Change in the Economic Status of Single Mothers under Welfare Reform*. Civic Report 35. New York: Manhattan Institute for Policy Research. http://www.manhattan-institute.org/html/ cr_35.htm.

Orbuch, T. L., Thornton, A., and Cancio, J. 2000. "The Impact of Marital Quality, Divorce, and Remarriage on the Relationships between Parents and Their Adult Children." *Marriage and*

Family Review 29 (4): 221–246.

Perloff, L. S. 1983. "Perceptions of Vulnerability to Victimization." *Journal of Social Issues* 39 (2): 41–61. doi: 10.1111/j.1540-4560.1983.tb00140.x.

Rohner, R. P., and Veneziano, R. A. 2001. "The Importance of Father Love: History and Contemporary Evidence." *Review of General Psychology* 5 (4): 382–405.

Seifert, K. L., Hoffnung, R. J., and Hoffnung, M. 2000. *Lifespan Development* (2nd ed.). New York: Houghton Mifflin.

Teyber, E. 1997. *Interpersonal Process in Psychotherapy: A Relational Approach.* Pacific Grove, CA: Brooks.

Tomkins, S. S. 1963. *The Negative Effects.* Vol. 2 of *Affect Imagery Consciousness.* New York: Tavistock/Routledge.

Ventura, S. J., and Bachrach, C. A. 2000. "Non-Marital Childbearing in the United States, 1940–1999." *National Vital Statistics Reports* 48 (16): 1–40.

Wade, B. 1995. "Fear of Abandonment." *Essence* 25 (2): 79–86.